Kicking ASSpergers:

One Meltdown at a Time

Jeremy Tolmie, Dave Ray
and Joel Mark Harris

 FriesenPress

One Printers Way
Altona, MB R0G 0B0
Canada

www.friesenpress.com

ISBN
978-1-03-912892-7 (Hardcover)
978-1-03-912891-0 (Paperback)
978-1-03-912893-4 (eBook)

1. BIOGRAPHY & AUTOBIOGRAPHY, PERSONAL MEMOIRS

Distributed to the trade by The Ingram Book Company

About the Book

"I was tired of feeling this way. I was tired of everything, and I just wanted it to end... What would happen if I lit the entire place on fire? What if I just stayed perfectly still and did nothing?"

Kicking ASSpergers is the triumphant memoir of one man's journey with autism and his quest for happiness and self-empowerment despite the many challenges life throws at him. Detailing his struggles with acute anxiety, depression, OCD, psychosis, suicidal ideation, as well as social stigma and medical bias, Jeremy Tolmie moves through his childhood, from the moment he was adopted by loving parents, through brutal school years being bullied and teased, and into adulthood, where he attempts to hold down a job, attend college, and live semi-independently. Over time, Jeremy starts to alienate the people in his life with his erratic and dangerous behaviour, and finds himself in and out of various living situations, including psych wards. When he meets Dave Ray, a home share provider, Jeremy starts to learn how to "trust the process" and how not to let autism rule his life.

Written with humour, honesty, and compassion, *Kicking ASSpergers* breaks down stigma and dismantles myths and assumptions about autism.

This unique voice tells an inspirational story of friendship, trust, and perseverance in the face of adversity.

About the Author

Jeremy Tolmie has written three previous books— *Living with Asperger's Syndrome, Living with Autism Spectrum Disorder*, and *Living on the Autism Spectrum*. His goal in sharing his story is to inspire hope in others with autism, and their families.

He lives in home share in Nanaimo, British Columbia.

Dave Ray passed away on July 9, 2021. He will be missed by all. He was 66 years old.

Table of Contents

There were early signs of Tolmie's autism: he had difficulty adhering to structures in kindergarten, for example, suggesting that he was a bit different. He was not officially diagnosed until the twelfth grade, though, at a time when little was known about the disorder. In the years that followed, he moved in and out of the medical system and struggled to find stability in school and at work. Through a home-share opportunity, he began to experience some breakthroughs in handling his condition.

With candid descriptions of Tolmie's emotions—he recalls feeling resentful when he was placed in a special education class, and lonely around other children--this is an intimate and compelling book that highlights the struggles of people with ASD. But it also includes evidence of joy: Tolmie remembers buying his parents dinner for the first time while he was living in the home-share arrangement; he is loving in describing time spent with his grandmother. Tolmie celebrates those who helped him, too, with special emphasis on his parents, who stood up for him to teachers and who helped him seek medical help. Thus, the book achieves a strong balance.

EDITH WAIRIMU (February 16, 2022)
By Foreword Clarion Review

Prologue

FEELING HIGHLY AGITATED, I was only vaguely aware of what I was doing. I turned off the movie I was watching—*Alien*—and sat there looking at the blank, dark screen.

I thought about the alien creature killing off the astronauts who were alone in space, billions of light years away from Earth. The alien slowly picking the men and women off, one by one. I knew how the astronauts felt because that was exactly how I was feeling at that moment. I was alone. Afraid. It was almost like something inside me was building up, trying to get out, getting ready to explode through my chest.

To try and rid myself of this sensation, I decided I would go have a shower. It seemed like an incredibly difficult journey. My light footsteps creaked against the wooden floor panels. One foot in front of the other.

I got to the bathroom where I ran the water, feeling the temperature under my hand as the water slid down my fingertips and into the tub. I took off my clothes, folded them neatly, placed them on the countertop, and stepped into the shower.

I hate having showers. I hate the water touching my skin, I hate the water touching my hair, but I hoped somehow this time would be different. I hoped that the water would feel refreshing, rejuvenating—that's what people often told me—but my sense of helplessness and panic only increased. I took deep breaths to try to calm myself down, but it wasn't working.

I knew I was different from everyone, but I couldn't put my finger on it. There had been countless doctors, each with his or her own opinion, prescribing a new medication. But with each visit I felt more frustrated and more alone.

Growing up, the other kids were mean to me. No matter what I did, they picked on me, beat me up, pushed me, and called me names. How different I was only became more apparent as I got older. The other kids seemed so normal. So regular. And here I was, feeling like an outsider.

The water kept coming down. I stayed put, not moving, not sure what I could do. Eventually, I turned the shower off, dried myself, and got dressed. I was still alone in the house. My parents were working and wouldn't be home for several hours. The house suddenly seemed eerie and lonely.

Once again, I was gripped by panic, only worse this time. I decided I could no longer go on like this. Things just kept getting worse and worse.

I pulled the BBQ from the porch, lifting it over the sliding glass door jam and into the kitchen. I got the jerry can for the lawnmower from the tool shed and poured the gas all across the living room. The room stank. All I had to do was light it. It would be incredibly easy.

I was tired of feeling this way. I was tired of everything, and I just wanted it to end. I felt completely alone. Nobody understood what I was feeling, not even my parents, or my nana, whom I loved dearly. I didn't want to disappoint her or cause her any pain.

What would happen if I lit the entire place on fire? What if I just stayed perfectly still and did nothing? Why not let the flames engulf me? Would the propane tank explode like it did in the movies? Did I really want to die that way?

CHAPTER 1:
The Preteen Years

I WAS BORN IN WINNIPEG, Manitoba, Canada, on December 27, 1981, and I am a direct descendant of the Honourable James McKay. If you're not acquainted with your Canadian history (and if you're not, I don't blame you), he was a fur trader and early settler of Manitoba. He is famous for negotiating early First Nations land treaties before being appointed to the legislature.

Although I might have come from a distinguished family, my birth was decidedly not. I was given up for adoption by my birth parents and lived in foster care for eighteen months until I was adopted by Bob and Terry Tolmie in 1983.

On our first visit, my soon-to-be parents, Bob and Terry, gave me a teddy bear. Somehow, I remember this stuffed bear very clearly. The bear was brown with black eyes and was about the size of my head. Bob and Terry must have been really smitten with me because I'm told it was one of the fastest adoption processes that ever took place.

Soon I was in my new home in Brandon, Manitoba. Not long after I had settled in, I got an ear infection. I cried a lot, but my parents couldn't figure out what was wrong. One morning my parents woke me up and there was blood on the pillow. My eardrum had burst. To this day, I still have a little bit of hearing loss in my right ear.

About a year later, my parents decided to start a new adventure and move to Nanaimo, British Columbia, where I now live. We rented a moving truck, and my dad drove it while I rode in our car with my mother. Along the way, I came down with heatstroke and had to be hospitalized in Kamloops. The doctor prescribed popsicles and cold showers. I thought popsicles were great—cold showers not so much!

My mother and I caught the ferry that would take us across to Vancouver Island, but my dad, who was trailing us in the rental truck, missed it. We had to sit at the ferry terminal on the other side and wait for my dad to catch the next ferry because we had all the money and the directions. After about four hours, we were reunited and found the apartment we had rented. My dad had to move all the furniture himself because my mother was sick with the flu. He then decided to go out and get pizza for dinner but got lost on his way back. Maybe not the most promising beginning, but we had arrived.

When I was adopted at eighteen months, I still wasn't walking, and crawled everywhere. But man, what a crawler I was! I had the best crab technique you've seen a kid use! Although the fact that I wasn't walking was a bit of a concern for my parents, they felt it was only a delay in my growth due to how difficult the first year of my life had been.

It wasn't until my family noticed me squinting at the television that they thought to get my eyes checked. The optometrist said I was legally blind, and on top of that, I had a lazy eye. No wonder I'd had trouble. Thankfully the glasses helped, and in no time, I was walking. A whole new world was opened up to me; I was so excited to explore everything.

I distinctly remember hearing my dad's voice and looking up at this man I had never seen before. I could clearly see the shape of his head, his cheekbones, and his big smile. I asked my mom if this was my daddy.

She smiled, teared up, and said that indeed he was. I was overjoyed and my parents became emotional. This was a very special moment in my early life!

I remember my dad reading nursery rhymes to me at bedtime. Although I could not read, I eventually memorized the words and would recite them with my dad. My dad thought I was advancing in my reading when in fact I just had a good memory.

Both my parents got jobs when we moved to Nanaimo and I was put in daycare, which I absolutely hated. I didn't like being around other kids because they were so much different than I was. I had trouble talking to them and relating to them. They seemed so much more advanced than I was. All I would do was run and hide. I also had this terrible fear that my new parents were going to leave me, and I would end up bouncing from foster parent to foster parent forever. I hated daycare so much my mother eventually had to quit her job at the bank in order to stay home with me.

I started kindergarten when I was four and there were already signs that I was antisocial and had difficulty following structure. The school thought it was best if I repeated kindergarten as my learning was delayed. I didn't quite understand what was going on, but I didn't mind. After all, I got to play with the train set again and take a nap every day. For a kid who didn't much like change, it was the lap of luxury.

The older I grew, the more I struggled to relate to the other kids, although I do remember playing with the girl downstairs. She and her family were tenants. I was around three or four years old at the time. She and I would play hide-and-go-seek and other games, and it was a lot of fun. She was very friendly and easy to talk to and play with. She was non-judgmental and just accepted me for who I was. I think that is why we got along so well, and we were friends until we moved to our permanent home in Nanaimo.

It became increasingly apparent that there was something very different about me, although nobody seemed to be able to tell me exactly what that was. I hated being different and just wished I could fit in with the other kids. Over the next couple of years, my school conducted some tests and concluded that I had learning disabilities, especially with Math and English.

Eventually my marks got so bad I was put into Special Education for English and Math. I managed to pull myself up, and in grade three I got my best marks ever. Going into grade four I felt fairly confident, but before I could prove myself, the teacher shipped me off to Special Ed again because she didn't want to deal with me. I deflated; I could feel my self-esteem plummet. For someone who had low self-esteem already, this really hurt. I remember slowly walking home after school that day, feeling especially dejected. I didn't tell my parents because I was so embarrassed.

In school, my resentment began to grow because all I wanted to do was learn, and in Special Ed I was never tested and didn't feel challenged. So instead of complaining, I wrote a story during the first half of grade four in which I discussed how I felt about the teacher who put me in the Special Ed class in the first place. I showed the story to my parents, and they immediately went to the principal and demanded that I be put back in regular classes. The school eventually agreed with my parents, and I went back to my regular classroom with all my friends. As I re-entered, students actually gave me a standing ovation. I was shocked. Apparently, none of the other kids liked the teacher either, and so I became a minor celebrity for a couple of days for being the kid who stood up against institutional tyranny.

Neither sports nor P.E. ever became any easier. I still hadn't developed any good hand-eye coordination, and my blindness prevented me from being able to do many of the activities other kids took for granted. One time, during grade seven, when I was in P.E. class, I overexerted myself and passed out.

My parents took me to the Children's Hospital in Vancouver for an overnight assessment. The doctors performed tests on my heart. I had to run on a treadmill for thirty minutes. Just as I was being unhooked from the machines, I had a massive asthma attack and almost passed out. I also had to run around Stanley Park with a heart monitor. Of course, I hated this entire experience because I didn't want to run. If I had known what was in store for me, I would have fought my parents tooth and nail to stay home. One thing I didn't realize was how many sick children there were, with cancer and other diseases, who may never be going home. This really opened my eyes.

The doctors diagnosed me with exercise-induced asthma. I used inhalers until the end of high school when I felt I didn't need them anymore. The one good thing that came out of that experience was that I was exempt from P.E. class.

During my elementary years I developed some friendships, though they were always initiated by the other kids because I was too afraid to approach them or talk to them. I didn't like being lonely, but the fear of talking to the other kids was even more debilitating, so when somebody initiated a conversation, I was at least willing to participate.

However, as I got older, I struggled to make new friends and retain the ones that I had. It didn't help that I was an awkward, gangly child with thick glasses and a lack of hand-eye coordination. In addition, I struggled to show emotion, so the other kids thought I was a little bit robotic.

I started getting bullied in grade four. This contributed a lot to my difficulties in school and with people in general. Most of the time I felt petrified the moment I left my house. My days were filled with anxiety until I came home again and felt safe with my parents. I suffered in silence for the longest time, too scared to say or do anything about it. My usual protective mechanism of crying, which had, up to this point, been effectively deployed with my parents, didn't work with these kids. I generally tried to be as quiet as possible, hoping nobody would notice me or care. Of course, this only made the bullying worse.

One time I was playing outside with the neighbourhood kids. The house next door was in the process of being built, and the other kids started to climb the rafters. I didn't want to be left alone, so I started to climb with them. I pulled my body up onto one of the beams but couldn't find a way to climb back down. I called out to the other kids to help me, but they just laughed and ran away. There I was, terrified, up on this wooden beam, high above the ground. I didn't know what to do and had visions of staying up there until it got dark. Thankfully, my mother, who had been keeping a close eye on us, came to investigate. She found me and helped me climb back down.

Midway through grade six the bullying was so bad I eventually told my parents. They went to the school, to the bullies' parents, and to the police. We even tried to get a restraining order against one of the particularly bad bullies, but strangely enough the bully said *I* was bullying *him*. This was completely ridiculous. One look at my skinny arms and tiny body and anybody could tell that I couldn't bully anyone. I was angry and upset and, of course, the restraining order went nowhere, and the bullying only got worse.

One time, the boy tripped me. I got so mad, I wanted to retaliate. Knowing I couldn't try a direct assault, I had to find a weak spot. His brother was standing next to him; I held up my backpack, readying it as a weapon. But the bully tripped me again before I could get to his younger brother. Epic failure! I went home once again defeated.

I had this one friend who flat out told me that he couldn't be friends with me at school because I wasn't popular enough, although if I wanted, we could hang out at home. I was okay with that because I took what I could get, but my mother was incensed. She told me that she wouldn't have this boy over unless he was friends with me at school as well.

For a few summers my parents put me into camp on Newcastle Island, and once on Salt Spring Island. I hated camp because I didn't get along with the other kids and we played a lot of sports and other outdoor activities that I wasn't particularly good at. The camp only made me feel like more of an outsider than I already felt. All the other kids had friends or made friends easily. Not me. I was shy and quiet and would count the days until I got to go home and sleep in my own bed.

When I was fourteen, I did a training program on Salt Spring to become a camp leader, and then the next year I did training in Nanaimo. I eventually abandoned my training when I realized that to be a good camp leader I would have to become a good people person.

Of course, not everything was doom and gloom during my early years. I have wonderful memories of some amazing birthdays. My birthday is December 27, so my parents always went out of their way to make me feel special and not just skip over it because it was so close to Christmas.

One birthday, my parents hired a clown to make animal balloons, and they made a videotape, which is now on YouTube. On my ninth birthday we started a tradition that continues to this day: my parents and I go for pizza and a movie. Other times we took road trips to see the Seattle Mariners ballgames, travelled to Disney World, and even visited Mexico.

During one trip to Seattle, we were sitting in front of the Space Needle, enjoying a beautiful day in the park. I was sitting with my dad while my mom was sitting at a table opposite us. For some reason, I became fascinated with the umbrella and began to fiddle with the lever. My dad kept telling me to stop playing with it, but of course I didn't listen to him. I rotated the lever a little further and before I knew it the umbrella had snapped closed, trapping us inside.

I thought my mother would come to rescue us, but she was too busy laughing! Thankfully a police officer came over and lifted the umbrella to allow for our escape. He didn't think it was very funny, however. "Stop goofing around," he told us before walking away. This only made my mother laugh harder!

A fond memory I have of Mexico is when the locals got a huge kick out of my red hair. This was my first taste of celebrity status!

For my eleventh birthday, we went tobogganing at a resort on Vancouver Island called Mt. Washington. I couldn't ski worth a damn but had fun going downhill on the toboggan. My parents thought this was funny and said they wished they had a video camera.

I started kickboxing at age eight as a way to protect myself and gain some confidence. I went for four-and-a-half years and really enjoyed it. While it didn't really protect me from the bullies, it did give me some confidence. I kickboxed until I was twelve, when we moved to Gabriola Island where there wasn't a facility for me to continue my training.

My parents also encouraged me to play sports, which I didn't particularly enjoy. My lack of hand-eye coordination made it a challenge to say the least! My parents put me in hockey when I was ten years old. I played with kids four years younger than I was because I wasn't good enough to play with kids my own age. I managed to last an entire season, which I thought was pretty good. Playing hockey didn't stick but my lifelong love of the Vancouver Canucks did. I started to collect the players' jerseys and managed to acquire a substantial collection, including Trevor Lindon's game 6 of the Stanley Cup final in 1994.

My father would sometimes get box seats to the Vancouver Canucks through work, and we would make the ferry trip across to Vancouver to watch the Canucks play. We would stay the night and make a whole day out of it. That was a real treat, although I hated the crowds and all the people. Thankfully, when I was watching the game, I could block it all out, but getting in and out of the stadium was a real problem. I suffered in silence because I didn't want to disappoint my parents.

I started to make up stories about playing soccer at lunchtime just to make my mom and dad happy. My stories were elaborate tales of how I would assist in a goal, make a great play, or help win the game. I became very good at lying, although my intention was never to hurt anyone. I just wanted to make my parents proud of me. Eventually, I confessed to them that I wasn't actually playing soccer during lunchtime and had made the whole thing up.

My mom stayed home with me until grade seven when she decided that was a good time to go back to work. In the back of my mind, I still had this nagging suspicion that my parents would somehow disown me or stop caring about me. Of course, my parents were the most loving people a kid could ask for, but I was still scared that I would end up alone. I became resentful and tried to make my parents' lives a living hell to convince them that I couldn't live without them.

I was a picky eater growing up, so my parents had to bribe me with Dairy Queen ice cream to make me eat my meals. It worked like a charm. If I was really uncooperative, the ante was raised to a Blizzard! How could I resist? Oreo Blizzard or bust! This technique also worked for doing outside activities, like five-pin bowling or swimming. I was in a bowling league for three years, and stuck with swimming for close to seven years, even getting to two levels behind a certified lifeguard.

My parents were really good to me. For example, I got an allowance for doing nothing until I was nine. Then all I had to do was my own laundry, set the table, and load and unload the dishwasher. I was making five dollars a week, which at the time felt like I was swimming in money. When I turned fourteen, I started to clean the house and water the plants. I got thirty dollars a week for my efforts.

One summer, when I was six, my parents took me camping near Osoyoos. We were having a picnic and we overheard the family adjacent to us saying they had just picked up a Nintendo for only ninety-nine dollars. This was much cheaper than anything we had seen in Nanaimo! My parents went over to ask them where they had gotten the Nintendo and they told us they had gotten it from the Safeway just across the border in the United States.

Perfect! We went across the border and bought the Nintendo with my own allowance money that I had been saving. I would play Duck Hunt and Mario Brothers after school; this gave me something to do. That first game console made me an avid gamer, and afterward I would get a new game every year for my birthday. At age ten I developed a huge interest in computers when my parents bought their first one. I was fascinated by their operating systems and what you could do with them. One of the best aspects of these technologies was that I didn't have to interact with people. I could play and tinker around to my heart's content.

I wanted to earn some more money so when I turned eleven, I got a paper route and went out a couple of times a week. I lugged the papers door-to-door using a wagon. My parents helped me when they could by loading and unloading my wagon. I'm not sure if it was because of my parents' help or if I was just a naturally good paperboy, but I won paperboy of the month twice and was nominated as paperboy of the year.

Occasionally, while I was out delivering papers, a bully would follow me and heckle me from afar. They would say, four eyes, loser, geek, nerd, just to name a few. The more the bullies bothered me, the more I withdrew and tried to hide. But I knew I couldn't hide in my bubble forever. As elementary school came to a close, I became more and more anxious about high school. What was awaiting me there? Whatever it was, I didn't think it would be good. The gap between me and the other kids only seemed to widen as I grew older.

CHAPTER 2:
The Adolescent Years

THOUGHT STARTING MY TEEN years with dozens of phone calls to Disney was a good idea. I came up with a new movie that I thought would make an excellent sequel to *The Lion King*. I wrote the script and got some of my friends to act it out. I even got them all to sign contracts!

I decided I would need some money in order to make this movie a reality, so I applied for a one-million-dollar loan from the local credit union. I put my nana down as a reference and then faxed it in. For some reason, I was denied!

My next move was to contact the head of the Thrifty Foods program—who was responsible for community projects—and ask if they could spare a million dollars for my movie idea. For some reason, I was denied there too!

I was, however, very persistent with my phone calls to Disney. I even managed to speak to the VP of Disney operations! Everybody I spoke to was very interested and listened politely to my presentation. I persisted with these phone calls, and I called them regularly for a whole month.

Eventually, my parents figured out what I was up to when they got a bill in the mail for $550 for all the phone calls I was making to the United States. I eventually got a letter from Disney explaining that they had their own team in place and were not interested in my sequel. They did suggest, however, that I might want to apply to the youth acting school. My parents were not keen on this idea and were more interested in knowing how I was going to repay them for the telephone bill. There is a strong probability that I still owe them.

To make matters worse, I now had a bunch of contract actors threatening to sue me for unpaid wages! I guess I just wasn't cut out for Hollywood.

I dearly loved my nana, although it's doubtful that she would have co-signed a loan for me. We would spend the holidays together, and she would get me great presents for my birthday. She would babysit me when my parents went out, and sometimes we would go golfing together on a nine-hole course. Although I didn't much care for golf, I enjoyed hanging out with my nana. She always cared about me and believed in me and never made me feel like I couldn't do something. She never treated me like anything other than a regular kid; she always made me feel like I was the most important and smartest person in the room.

One of the more memorable times is when my nana and I drove down to Tucson, Arizona, and stayed there for two weeks. My nana was staying for another week, so I had to fly home by myself. I didn't hear the announcement that only kids aged 12 and under would be escorted off of the plane and I was 13 by that time. So I almost didn't get off when I should have. If I had stayed on, I would have gone to Alaska!

During this time, Vancouver was awarded an NBA team called the Vancouver Grizzlies, and I became an instant fan. I bought a Vancouver Grizzlies winter parka and a basketball—which would now be considered collectors' items. Sadly, the franchise only lasted six seasons when they were sold to Memphis.

I had started skipping school in grade seven and as a result, before I started high school, my parents enrolled me in summer school. They hoped it would prepare me for the upcoming year. They knew that the transition to high school would be difficult, and they wanted to make it as smooth as possible.

I was enrolled in Math and English, and while this helped some, it did not lessen my growing anxiety about high school. The travel to and from school alone was very stressful. We had moved from Nanaimo to Gabriola Island, a small island just east of Nanaimo with a population of a few thousand people, linked to Nanaimo by a twenty-minute ferry ride.

From an early age I found I didn't like change and hated moving—and I do mean *hate*! Now I had to take a ferry ride followed by a bus to the high school in Nanaimo. This required me to get up at six-thirty in the morning in order to get ready, eat breakfast, and make my lunch to catch the 7:50 boat so as not to miss my bus. And then I had to book it to the bus stop after school so I could be home at four-thirty. If I missed my bus, I wouldn't be home until after six, and I would have to contend with the bullies while I waited for the next one. I would find myself in class, not listening to a word the teacher was saying because I was so anxiously awaiting the final bell. Sometimes on the bus the other kids wouldn't let me sit by them, and I would have to stand the entire way.

High school was very different from elementary. For starters, in elementary you stayed with the same teacher and classroom, while in high school you have four periods a day and have to shuffle between classrooms. I had four different teachers every day and of course they changed halfway through the year as I was on a semester schedule. Plus, the order of the classes changed so I had to remember where I had to be on a specific day. This was extremely stressful and difficult. Eventually, I kind of got used to this routine, but I always had some level of anxiety trying to figure out where I was supposed to be.

Unfortunately, I still had the same one bully to contend with. He must've felt it was his duty to continue my torment. He would chase me around school daily, and I would have to run for my life.

I continued going to Special Ed classes for Math and English but participated in my regular classes for the rest of the subjects. I struggled in school, and my marks were consistently below average but apparently good enough to pass.

Unfortunately, I was back in P.E., where I got my first detention in grade eight (amazingly enough, it was my first and only detention in high school). The P.E. teacher thought I was not paying attention, so he decided to throw a basketball at me. Due to my lack of hand-eye coordination and my sight issues, I missed the ball and it bounced straight off my head.

One would think the teacher would've been sympathetic, but instead he got even angrier and gave me a detention for not paying attention. I told my parents, and they were extremely angry. They went straight to the principal and asked for the teacher to be reprimanded. I don't know what consequences the teacher faced but I do know that I never had any further problems with him. It was not until grade nine that I found out I needed two doctors' notes to be exempt from P.E.

Although grade eight was a struggle, I still managed to just barely pass all my courses. I was extremely lonely and felt very isolated from the other kids who wouldn't talk to me because they thought I was weird. My social anxiety increased, and though I desperately wanted to make friends, I was too scared to approach anyone.

Thankfully, at the beginning of grade nine, my Special Ed teacher introduced me to a guy named Aron, a fellow student who had moved to Gabriola Island at the start of the school year. In fact, we lived just a few blocks apart. Aron was a big, broad-shouldered, six-foot-three, 240-pound behemoth. We began to travel to and from school together and spend time hanging out. My anxiety about catching the school bus lessened, as I now had someone to sit with. Aron and I became virtually insepa-rable. We both enjoyed video games and when we weren't playing them, we were talking about them. We played a variety of games. A couple of them were "Need for Speed" and "Duke Nukem."

An additional advantage to being friends with Aron was that the bully took one look at Aron's massive frame and decided to take up another hobby! Aron looked intimidating, but he was actu-ally very quiet and gentle. In school or large groups, he was fairly quiet, but when he was comfortable, he would open up and talk. Aron became my best buddy—and not just because he scared away the bully. I think I can safely say he's the reason I made it through high school alive.

I attended high school fairly regularly, though I pretended to be sick many times so I could stay home. Sometimes it worked, but more often than not my parents sent me anyways. I played hooky from my band class in grade nine because I was so anxious about the exams. I played the trombone and did not think I was good enough to pass. Part of band class included going to practice after school, but I stopped going to that as well. Of course, my parents eventually found out. Thankfully, they supported me, and I was able to drop out of music. The school gave me a free period where I could do homework for my other courses.

Aron and I joined a bowling league in grade nine, and every Saturday we would go bowling and to a movie. We did the bowling league for two years. I know that I would not have done any of those things by myself. I was so grateful to have a real friend!

Aron had gone to Shawnigan Lake school but had flunked out, so he was behind a year. The teachers put him in an accelerated program in hopes that he would catch up to his classmates and graduate when he was supposed to. The school always wanted Aron to play rugby or football because he was so big, but Aron did not like physical contact or verbal altercations of any kind. He was really a gentle giant.

When I was in grades seven and eight, I tried my hand at entrepreneurship. Pogs was a popular game at the time, where you flipped these circular cardboard pieces, and if you won you got to keep your opponent's Pog. The Pogs came in all sorts of different colours and patterns and were collected by kids of all ages. I thought I could make some money buying, selling, and trading them.

One time I was at home with my parents, and this car pulled up with a mother and two kids. They knocked on our door and when my dad answered, the mother asked, "Is this Jeremy's Pog Shop?"

My parents just looked at me with raised eyebrows.

"Yes it is," I said quickly. I ran to the garage got out the sign I had made to show them. I sold the kids the Pogs and made a little bit of cash. Although I did make some money, this entrepreneurship was short-lived.

On my sixteenth birthday, I went and took the test for my learner's licence. I passed but was really very anxious about getting my full licence. I took a driver's course in the summer, and my parents took me driving many times to help me learn. My parents were great teachers, but I do believe that my mom was more nervous than my dad. I once hit a dog, which scared the bejesus out of me, but thankfully the dog wasn't seriously hurt. I took my first driver's test but did not pass. I took the test a few more times but never got my licence. I eventually came to accept my driving challenges and I am at peace with not having a licence.

I was good with directions, though. One time my mother stayed behind with my nana while my dad and I drove to Phoenix with our dog Nemo. The first night of our trip we stayed in Tacoma, Washington, without any hitches. The next day, my birthday, we stayed in a town called Red Bluff, California. My dad and I had dinner at Applebee's, where the staff sang "Happy Birthday" to me. The following day we arrived in an area called Grapevine, which is just north of Los Angeles. Next, we came over the hill and drove right into L.A. As we were sitting in rush hour traffic, it started to monsoon. Even with the windshield wipers on full blast, it was challenging for my dad to see clearly. Now, even with my limited driving experience, I knew that Nanaimo traffic was no comparison to the challenge it was to drive on L.A.'s gigantic freeways during rush hour. My dad, knowing that I was good with maps, put me in charge of navigating. At home he had printed out a couple of Google maps to get us to our destinations. I studied the maps and managed to get us to our hotel—which was in a town called Ontario, California—without any difficulty. My dad was pretty stressed, but we still managed to walk across the street to a Mexican restaurant, where he proceeded to gulp down three margaritas! We ate dinner, went back to the motel, passed out, and slept till morning. On the last leg we made it to Phoenix and began our vacation. The next day my mom flew down to meet us and we picked her up at the Mesa Airport.

When I was twenty years old, I went back to Winnipeg for one week to visit my birth grandmother and my birth brother. I was incredibly anxious about this visit, and my anxiety only got worse as it got closer. My birth grandmother was incredibly generous, however, and she really tried to make up for lost time. We went to The Keg for dinner with my biological brother and we exchanged stories and I got some insight into my biological parents. I didn't stay in contact with my birth brother, but my birth grandmother sent me a birthday present every year until she died.

My parents also took me to a *Star Trek* convention in Las Vegas. We flew there, and of course I was terrified of the takeoff and the landing, but once we were in the air, I was alright. This would be the first of three trips we took to Las Vegas. The second trip was for my cousin's wedding, and the third trip was just to go on vacation.

The first trip to Las Vegas was my favourite one because we went to the *Star Trek* convention. I watched my first ever *Star Trek* episode with my dad and to this day I am an avid Trekkie. I have numerous *Star Trek* collectibles and own all of their movies and TV episodes, which I have watched numerous times. While at the convention in 2002, I purchased a Captain Kirk *Star Trek* uniform jacket for $700 and a bomber-style jacket for around $200.

I went on my first rollercoaster ride when I was in Vegas, which was an absolutely terrifying experience. The attendants made me take off my glasses and hold them so I couldn't even see what was happening. The roller coaster went from one of the bottom floors of a hotel and wrapped around the building all the way to the top before going back down backwards. The rollercoaster went up and down twice before I could get off. I was not a fan! Afterwards my legs were so jelly-like I could barely walk.

Rollercoasters notwithstanding, these types of vacations were a great way for me to escape reality for a while. My anxiety had been building steadily in my first couple of high school years. This is when I really began to see life differently and I was fighting with my inner turmoil and my general outlook. Ultimately, high school was not a great place for my overall well-being. I just couldn't cope with the constant stress and anxiety that it caused. I had a nervous breakdown at the end of 1998 and went to the psych ward for three weeks. Not long after I got out, I dropped out of school. I was midway through grade eleven.

It got to a point where I didn't want to deal with reality anymore and started to have thoughts about ending my life. Being friends with Aron was a big help. Aron was somebody I bonded with because he had similar challenges. He really struggled in school as well, and the teachers basically rushed him through the system, even if he didn't pass all his grades.

Although I couldn't exactly say what it was, I knew I was different, and my fear prevented me from making any changes. I was stuck without any alternatives. I tried desperately to hide my feelings from everyone, but my actions would soon expose me to the world.

CHAPTER 3:
All Hell Breaks Loose

I N AUGUST 1998, MY parents received a fateful phone call that would change the direction of my life. It was from my biological grandmother, who informed my parents that my birth mother had passed away from a brain tumour. In the same conversation, she suggested that I get tested for possible mental health issues that ran in my family.

I knew very little about my birth family, but we did learn from my biological grandmother that she had taken my biological mom to the Mayo Clinic for testing, where she had been diagnosed with schizophrenia. I also learned that social services had removed me from my mom's home before I was placed in foster care and then later adopted.

Following the phone call from my grandmother, my parents took me to see a psychiatrist who diagnosed me with obsessive-compulsive disorder (OCD) and prescribed Paxil and Anafranil after only a single consultation.

I knew I displayed some OCD-like behaviour; for example, I would always line up the TV remotes, or I'd get angry when people rested their arms a certain way. But I didn't feel the diagnosis was entirely accurate; I didn't think it explained my anxiety or social awkwardness. I never really discussed any of this with my parents, who were doing their absolute best to follow the psychiatrist's suggestions. They thought it was best for me.

I had been on the medication for about three months when I started to suffer from significant acne. I went to a dermatologist who prescribed me Accutane. Unfortunately, I had an allergic reaction to the medication, but the doctors encouraged me to keep monitoring it and the dosage was, in fact, raised.

I had no way of knowing that the OCD medication along with the acne medication were causing adverse effects. I started to have psychotic episodes and some really dark thoughts, seeing things that weren't there, and I also had thoughts about killing myself. Not realizing that it was the medication,

I tried to manage it by myself, but slowly things got worse and worse. Compounding this problem was the fact that I kept my feelings and images to myself. I was too afraid and embarrassed to tell my parents or the psychiatrist the truth.

I started to become compulsive, not really thinking things through. On numerous occasions I ran away from home and hid in the bush. One time I even took our dog and walked halfway around Gabriola Island, which would be equal to about seven kilometres. I would often stay hidden until my parents would find me.

My depression was getting worse and so was my acne, so the dermatologist increased the dosage of the Accutane, and the psychiatrist increased the Paxil dosage. I also wasn't sleeping, so they put me on some sleep medication, but I developed a tic, so they gave me something else. Every time they changed my medication or the dosage, my behaviour got worse.

It was around this time that my parents became suspicious of my behaviours and started to think that the medications were not right for me. My parents would fight with the psychiatrist, saying there was something wrong with the medications, but she wouldn't listen.

Before Christmas, the school was offering free computers to students. These computers were significantly outdated, worse than the one I already had at home, but a free computer seemed like a good idea. I decided to steal one of their better computers, which was still not quite as good as the one I had at home but was better than the ones they were offering for free. I didn't really think anybody would notice one computer missing. At this point, my thoughts were getting more and more chaotic, and I felt I couldn't help myself. The theft was discovered almost immediately (but not before I'd installed Windows 95 on it!). Luckily for me, the high school thought I had taken the computer by mistake, so I simply returned it without any consequences.

Shortly after this, I staged a burglary into my parents' house by smashing the side door and computer room door with a sledgehammer I had found in the carport storage shed. I stole everything I could get my hands on, including the computer, stereo, and some money. I also removed half of the RAM chips from the computer before I took it from the house. I tried to steal their television, but it was too heavy for me. Not really thinking anything through, I decided to hide everything in a vacant forested lot next door. I didn't really have any type of plan. I stole the stuff just because. When I was finished hiding everything, I called the police to report the break-in.

I thought I was pretty clever, but it was just my luck that it snowed that night and when I went to check on the stuff the next morning, my mom discovered my footprints in the snow and traced them to the stash of stolen goods. I realized then I probably should have come up with a better plan!

My mom thought these were the footprints of the robber and called to tell the police that they had found their stuff. I began to panic when the police took all our fingerprints. That evening I tried to steal the computer again but this time my mom caught me in the act. I was busted. My mom asked if I had broken into the house, and I admitted to it.

She notified the police and told them everything. Thankfully there were no charges laid, but the police suggested I might need some counselling. I never went to counselling because I didn't think it would help.

I knew I was spiralling out of control but also felt like there was nothing I could do to stop it. All sorts of thoughts bombarded my brain.

Sometime around New Year's Eve, I was replacing the RAM chips from my parents' computer. I turned the computer on, but something went wrong, and I fried the motherboard. This caused me to have a nervous breakdown; I couldn't stop crying and shaking. I curled up on the floor trying to shut everything out, including my parent's voices. I scared my parents enough that they took me to the hospital. I was admitted to the psychiatric ward and was there for three weeks. My mother had a hard time dealing with the situation and rarely visited me. She didn't want to see me in a place like that. My dad, however, would come see me and we would take short walks around the hospital grounds. I have vague memories of this time of my life, as the medications they put me on kept me in constant brain fog.

However, I do remember one time I was watching *Regis and Kathie Lee* when one of the other patients wanted to change the channel. I told her no, and we started to argue. We ended up in a tug-of-war, wrestling the remote from each other's control. Although it may seem ridiculous, I attempted to hide it up my sleeve. Nobody was seriously hurt, and the other patient went off to tell the hospital staff. Luckily the staff backed me up, and I was allowed to continue watching my program until it was over.

I was assessed while I was there, and the psychiatrist decided that I demonstrated schizophrenic tendencies, social phobia, OCD, and anxiety disorders. She continued with the Paxil medication but switched the Anafranil to Risperdal. My anxiety, however, continued to mount. I watched as other people did the simplest things and was amazed because these things continued to fill me with so much dread that I felt like it was drilling into my skull.

The meltdowns continued. In the beginning of the year, I had two more stints in the psych ward. The medication constantly made my brain foggy, so much of the time I was unaware of what I was doing or what was going on around me.

During one of these visits, I was given a shot of Haldol, which caused me to go into a seizure. Although I did not lose consciousness, I did have violent muscle contractions, and my head bounced uncontrollably off the pillow. They gave me a shot of Ativan to counteract the seizure, and I remained in the hospital bed in the hallway for three days before they sent me home.

I wasn't getting any better no matter what the psychiatrist did, and in May my parents decided to send me to a thirty-day assessment in a hospital in Victoria that specialized in youth mental health. I didn't want to go because I hated being away from my family. When I arrived at the hospital, I was taken off all my meds so they could do a proper assessment.

I hated the stale environment, the terrible food, and the uncomfortable beds. I would get into fights with the other patients over the television. I begged the doctors to let me go home for the weekend and to put me back on Paxil. He agreed to put me back on the Paxil but didn't allow me to go home for the weekend since I didn't show any signs of improvement. When they told my dad I was not coming home for the weekend, he told them I would find a way to escape. The staff told him not to worry because they had all the security necessary to prevent me from escaping. By this time, I had been in and out of the medical system so many times, I didn't have much faith in any of the doctors and nurses. I thought, *what do they know?*

I was determined to get out of there. The hospital was supposed to be high security but escaping from it was surprisingly easy. I knew when the shift changes were and timed it accordingly. I just walked out. I was only stopped once by a security guard who asked if I had a hall pass. I replied that I did and that I was just going for a short walk and would be back shortly. I thought that the guard might ask to see my hall pass, but he just let me go.

I walked straight out the front door. I was planning to walk from Victoria to Nanaimo, which would have taken me at least twenty-four hours. I got about eighteen kilometres before, thankfully, I was picked up by a man who mistakenly thought he knew me and offered to take me to Nanaimo. I only had seven dollars on me, which I gave to him for gas when we stopped at the gas station. After leaving the gas station, we actually passed the bus that my mom was on, which was heading to Victoria where she was going to meet my dad! Of course, I didn't know that at the time.

By the time I had reached Nanaimo it was dark, and all I could think about was making the ferry to my home on Gabriola Island. I had to talk the ferry worker into letting me on to the last ferry—I had no money to pay. She must've felt sorry for me, or just recognized me and knew my situation.

As luck would have it, the ferry captain was getting off shift when we arrived on Gabriola, and he knew my parents were in Victoria to meet me, so he drove me home.

By the time my mom and dad reached the hospital in Victoria, I had already been gone for at least five hours. As expected, this did not surprise my dad, but my mom was pissed off.

My parents didn't think there was any way I could have gotten back to Nanaimo and so they desperately searched downtown Victoria for me. Now, although Victoria is a relatively small city and is generally a lovely place, it can get pretty seedy at nighttime in places and so my poor dad was asking anyone he came across—gang members, homeless people, drug addicts—if they had seen me.

One guy, a drug dealer or a gang member, even told my dad, "You're asking the wrong people."

My dad just shrugged helplessly and said, "Well, if you see him, could you tell the police?"

The guy shook his head. "We don't talk to the police."

My dad kept searching and eventually returned to the same spot where that same guy was standing. He seemed genuinely concerned and even asked my dad if he had found me.

Meanwhile, I finally reached home around midnight, using the spare key to get in. I called the hospital to tell my parents that I was home. They called my parents' hotel to give them the message.

I was famished because I hadn't eaten anything all day and was able to find food in the cupboard. After eating, I just went to bed as if nothing even happened. It had been a long day, but I was happy to be out of the hospital, even if it only lasted a little while.

My parents came home Saturday morning, slightly worried but not altogether surprised that I had managed to escape. They were just thankful that I had managed to somehow make it home safely. It was a very quiet weekend, and my parents returned me to the hospital Monday morning. My parents made me promise not to make any more escape attempts, and I fulfilled that promise.

Eventually, I managed to complete my thirty-day assessment. The team of doctors and medical staff concluded that I had pervasive developmental disorder, which is now known as autism spectrum disorder level 2. At the time, autism wasn't as well-known as it is today, and there was little in the way of help for people like me. There was the Autism Society of BC, but we did not know of its existence because it hadn't been made clear enough to my parents or myself that I had autism. Today there are all types of resources and information available, but that wasn't the case back then. My parents and I were left to figure it out on our own.

One person who still refused to treat me any differently was my nana. She continued to treat me as if I was a regular kid. I really loved her because she was always an advocate for me.

When I returned home, we went to see my psychiatrist in Nanaimo. She didn't know anything about autism or pervasive developmental disorder. She once again altered my meds from Paxil to Zoloft and kept me on the Risperdal. By this time, I knew that the Paxil wasn't helping and was in fact probably contributing to my behaviour problems. Zoloft is generally used to treat depression, panic attacks, and obsessive-compulsive disorder. And although I had displayed all the symptoms, the psychiatrist wasn't getting to the root of the problem, which was my autism.

Not surprisingly, none of the medications helped, and I continue to spiral, getting more depressed and more anxious with each passing day. My thoughts and feelings were erratic, and I had a hard time focusing. I also became more compulsive. I convinced my dad to buy me a DVD player for my computer so I could watch movies. I took a pencil to it, marking it up so it couldn't be returned. My parents decided that I would have to pay off the DVD player before I could use it. I was making thirty dollars in allowance, and it cost five hundred dollars. As you can imagine, it took me a while to pay it off!

Sometime in June 1999, I decided to sell my computer and purchase a Discman and the *Alien* movie collection. I had no idea what I was doing or the reasons behind my actions. I didn't even really like any science fiction movies other than *Star Trek* and *Star Wars*. A thought appeared in my mind, and I acted on it. It was that simple.

My thoughts and feelings kept getting darker. My mind kept going off the rails and suicidal tendencies started to creep in. I started to wonder what it would be like to just end it all and not have to go through the daily torment.

One time I went to my parent's bedside. I woke my dad and told him I was having a battle with the knife, and the knife was winning.

I didn't realize how scared this made my parents feel. Afterwards, my mom barricaded herself in the bedroom while my dad slept in the living room. Something good did come from this situation—at least for me. When I couldn't sleep, I would stay up with him.

My parents could see I wasn't doing very well and decided that one of them had to quit their job to stay home with me. But the psychiatrist advised against it, saying that I had to work out my problems on my own. To say that was bad advice might have been the understatement of the year!

My thoughts were erratic, and my mind was a mess. It's hard to explain what exactly I was thinking, but it was kind of like watching a movie of myself, feeling the anxiety and the panic, yet helpless to do anything but stare, far removed from the situation.

In July, my anxiety increased to astronomical levels. I kind of felt like an engine that was revved to maximum all the time. I decided I couldn't stand it anymore. I moved the BBQ into my parents' living room. I retrieved my dad's jerry can from the tool shed, went back inside the house, and doused the living room floor with gasoline and lit it on fire. The flames began to grow. Then I turned the propane tank on, waiting for the propane tank to explode. The shrill hiss of the compressed gas filled my ears. I watched as the room began to burn, wondering if I should just stand there until the smoke or the flames killed me.

Those few moments seemed to slow down. Even though my mind was all jumbled, I thought about my parents and about my nana and wondered what they would do if I was gone. Thankfully, I had put my cat in the rabbit cage in the backyard, far away from the house (not so thankfully for the rabbit, however, who had a heart attack and died). I wondered what it would be like to not have to deal with the constant anxiety and fear all the time. To be free of it all. But at the last moment, I decided to take the dog for a walk as the house began to burn. The dog was in his pen when I went to get him to take him for a walk. His pen was far enough from the house that he really was in no danger from the fire, but I took him anyways just to be safe.

I wasn't sure where I was going or what I was doing. My legs were just on autopilot while my mind felt like it was being stretched in all directions. I wasn't sure what route I took. All I know was when I returned home, the fire department and police were already at the scene. The neighbour had called 911 when she saw the flames from her house.

A police officer approached me and asked me to wait in his car while he sorted things out. The officer allowed me to put my dog in his pen, which was far enough away from the fire, and then I sat in his car. I waited for the police officer to return. My mind was still such a mess that I hadn't quite processed what I had done or the damage I had caused. The sheer magnitude of the situation did not hit me until I got to the police station.

The police drove me to the station where they put me in a waiting room. I don't remember how long I was there, but it seemed like an eternity. To use a *Star Trek* analogy, my brain was in warp speed. I was thinking about a thousand different scenarios, my anxiety getting worse and worse. I wondered what would happen to me. I was scared and frightened but also just tired. I decided that it didn't matter what happened to me anymore. I would accept whatever came my way.

My parents arrived at the station, and we spoke. They were frantic and scared but also concerned about me. I admitted to them that I had set the fire. The police decided that rather than being thrown in jail, I should be taken to the hospital and admitted to the psych ward.

I don't remember much those first few days in the ward. I do remember that I was feeling paranoid. I would constantly scan the room I was in, making sure nobody could get at me. I thought somebody was out to hurt me, and I should be ready.

After I burned down my parent's house, my relationship with them obviously became very strained. They of course wanted what was best for me, but they were unsure about what to do with me. Everything up to that point had proved to be a disaster. Of course, I don't blame them. They had just lost everything in the house fire, and insurance wouldn't cover it because I had set it on purpose. My parents had put their faith in the system, yet the system was failing us. The police convinced them that the best thing they could do was charge me with arson so I could at least get the help that I needed.

I remained in the psych ward until my first court appearance. The judge decided to send me to the Victoria Youth Detention Centre. During this time, the doctors couldn't get me my medication. I had to go cold turkey. But a strange thing happened, I started to feel better when I wasn't on anything. The fog lifted. Although I was still experiencing high anxiety, I had fewer dark thoughts.

I was only in Victoria for three days before I was sent to the youth facility in Burnaby for another thirty-day assessment. I was extremely scared and unsure what was happening to me. How was it possible that I was being charged with arson? It all seemed somehow surreal. It was only after my thoughts became clearer that I realized the severity of the situation. I didn't belong in the detention centre with the others. I wasn't a criminal ... was I? I felt like it had all been a horrible accident and was not my fault. The medication had made me go out of my mind, had made me burn down my parents' house. It wasn't something I would ever normally do.

The detention centre was a very depressing place, and I really missed my parents, although they did make one trip to visit me. They remarked how much I had changed since being off my medication. I didn't like being so far away from home and constantly thought about being reunited with them. It didn't dawn on me that they probably didn't want me back home and were going through their own struggles with the loss of their house.

I have to say the corrections officers were extremely nice to me, even when I didn't perform some of the tasks correctly, like mopping the floor. I was also allowed to opt out of the sports as I still disliked any physical activities.

Following the thirty-day assessment, I was sent back to court. The report given to the judge stated that there was nothing wrong with me and I was fit to stand trial. My parents and I were shocked at the outcome. My parents were frustrated because they felt the police had given them some bad advice. If convicted, I could be facing some serious jail time and would be treated as a criminal, not someone who needed help.

Thankfully, I was put on probation until the trial. My parents were extremely frustrated and decided to hire a lawyer for any further court appearances and the upcoming trial. This was a further cost to my parents, who had already lost everything in the fire.

For the first couple of months, we had nowhere to live. My parents stayed in a camper trailer while I slept in a cardboard box under a mosquito net. I didn't actually mind this as I thought of it as a fun adventure. And I was back with my parents, even though things were strained between us.

At this time, I was still off my medications. My parents noticed a change in my behaviour, and this was the beginning of the time when they suspected that it was, in fact, the medication that had caused me to become unstable. We went back to my psychiatrist. She abruptly told us that I was no longer one of her patients and couldn't treat me. Confused and angry, we walked out without any guidance or inkling of what to do next.

In September, my parents and the lawyer decided I needed to return to Victoria for another thirty-day assessment. My lawyer hoped that if we could prove I had a mental illness, I wouldn't be put on trial. I had seemed to be my normal self, without any more meltdowns or behavioural issues. My parents became even more convinced that the medication had contributed to my downfall, and I still had not been diagnosed properly.

The Victoria hospital agreed to take me in again since they believed I needed to be locked up in a mental institution. The doctors even told my parents to drop me off in downtown Victoria and let the system take care of me. But of course, my parents wouldn't ever think of doing that.

I was there for forty-five days. By this time, I had been off my meds for a while and didn't show any psychotic symptoms. The staff wanted more time to get a diagnosis in place. They concluded that I definitely had autism, pervasive developmental disorder. One neurological psychologist was convinced that I had Asperger's. Although Asperger's is no longer an acceptable term due to Doctor Asperger's connection to the Third Reich, it is still the one diagnosis I most identify with. It's now known as ASD Level 1. The doctors gave my parents information about how to get into contact with the Autism Society of BC, which would give me the support I needed.

Meanwhile, my lawyer and parents were building a case to get me better support. My dad requested all of my medical files and put together a chart that showed how my bad reactions to the medication coincided with all my behavioural problems. The chart covered two-and-a-half years and demonstrated very accurately how my behaviour was drastically altered by the medications I took. This was key to my defence and was shared with the Crown lawyer who was able to substantiate this with medical doctors.

Once again, I was in court, where the report from Victoria explained what my condition was. Based on this report, the prosecution could see that I was not a criminal and in fact did have a mental disability. He recommended that the charges be dropped, and I was free to go. I was overjoyed. I felt a great relief that I wasn't going to be sent to prison.

I was able to get the help I needed. Through the Autism Society of BC, I was able to get disability assistance, a disability bus pass, a ferry pass, an entertainment pass (my favourite), and a tax credit.

However, shortly after this court appearance, my parents sent me to a youth group home in Nanaimo. I did not want to go, but my parents thought that there needed to be consequences for my actions, and that a youth home would help me. When we first arrived, I locked all the doors of the car and refused to come out. It took quite a lot of convincing to get me to even consider the idea. I tried to convince them to take me home with them, but they used their extraordinary bribery skills and offered me a new laptop computer if I agreed to go.

CHAPTER 4:
Early Adult Years

HATED THE TIME I spent in the group home. Everything was so foreign to me, and I missed the familiarity of my home and routine. I was in a constant state of anxiety and experienced numerous meltdowns. I was extremely upset with my parents for making me move into the group home and I didn't understand why they wouldn't let me back into the house with them.

Although I appeared to be thinking and acting more clearly, I was starting to show signs of extreme anxiety, which resulted in psychotic meltdowns. Eventually, it would become apparent that I had two conditions: Asperger's autism and mild schizophrenia. In time, I would try to make my second condition seem much worse than it was.

Many of the other teens in the group home reacted violently towards the staff or the other residents. There was constant fighting and disturbances, which of course made everything extremely difficult and caused me continuous anxiety. For much of my time there, I felt utterly alone. I didn't feel like I could talk to anybody about my anxiety or how I was feeling.

The house had four bedrooms and a den that was converted into an office for the staff. As was my usual behaviour, I kept a low profile and didn't interact with the other residents.

I would get up at seven a.m. and make my own breakfast and lunch. On weekends the other residents would go home, but I would only go home every second weekend, which meant I was often the only one there. I would be sent to the grocery store with some money and had to cook for the aide and myself. I had never really fended for myself before, so in a way this experience, although dreadful, taught me how to cook, shop, and budget.

On the weekends with my parents, I would take the ferry over to Gabriola Island where our house had been rebuilt. I felt sad that I could only see my parents every other weekend, but at this point they were still angry and burnt out from the entire ordeal. Considering everything I had done,

I should have realized that visits with them were not my right, they were a privilege. At this point, it still had not dawned on me the extent of the pain and suffering I had caused my parents, and the thousands of dollars of damage I had done. My fear and anxiety prevented me from thinking about other people and only about myself all the time. My denial was getting stronger with each day, yet my parents were still in my corner, supporting me one hundred percent, even though it must've been tough for them to do so.

I was letting my autism and my anxiety take hold of my life, and all my decisions were fear-based. I was missing some of life's basic skills, like how to buy my parents cards or gifts. I never told them that I loved them without them prompting me first.

My new psychiatrist wanted to put me on more medication, but I refused. I still didn't trust any doctors and thought they were a bunch of frauds. My parents supported that decision because they saw in the past how the medications made me react. The psychiatrist promptly fired me as a patient because I wouldn't listen to his instructions. But that was okay with me because I didn't have any faith in him anyways.

Despite all this, I managed to go back to high school and complete grade eleven Social Studies, Earth Science, and Keyboarding.

I also managed to make one unlikely friend at the group home, named Kin. We would talk about music and play computer games. Kin couldn't read or write and went to a special school. Kin would get into fights with the staff and was constantly trying to find ways to push the boundaries by playing his music too loudly or by being disruptive.

Kin and I never fought, though, and I didn't care about any of his anger issues. I was just happy to have a friend who took me under his wing and protected me from the other residents—not that I had any particular trouble with anybody, although one resident went off the handles once and tried to attack me. Thankfully, Kin was there to stand up for me. The police were called on this resident, and the situation was eventually resolved.

I played games on my laptop, and then eventually I requested Internet access. They gave in but would only allow me two hours per day on the computer, which I was extremely unhappy about.

It wasn't all bad. I was able to go to the movies every Tuesday, and once a week I would volunteer to walk the dogs at a local pet shelter. I even helped them construct an addition on the shelter.

After the torturous year was up, I had to move out as I was too old to stay in the youth home. I was still campaigning to move back home, but my parents weren't completely convinced. By this time, with the help of some friends in the construction trades, my parents had fully rebuilt the house.

We looked at an adult group home, but the residents there were very low functioning. In the end, my parents and I decided that it wasn't the right fit. I was coming home!

I was still able to attend many of the day programs run by the youth home, which included helping out at a horse ranch where I fed and took care of the horses. I also got to ride these horses and do tricks with them.

I started volunteering at a used bookstore in June 2001 and oversaw the sci-fi section, which I enjoyed. The used bookstore eventually hired me from May to September of 2002 to refurbish used computers that went to underprivileged children in Nanaimo.

I got a scholarship from the Autism Society of BC to attend vocational training and attended a computer technician class where I got my diploma to build and repair computers. I still loved computers and was good with them.

After my graduation I was given a contract by a company to replace cash registers at local cinemas and computers at local banks. This company also offered me the Nanaimo computer technician job for an international computer company, but for reasons unknown to me, this never came to fruition.

During this time, because of my legal troubles and emotional state, I had limited contact with my best friend Aron, but halfway through the vocational course, we reconnected. His friendship meant a lot to me as he was really my only true friend. My social phobia was still preventing me from attending any social functions, and talking to new people was extremely anxiety-producing, so making friends was next to impossible. Having Aron in my life really helped me.

My parents decided to convert the carport into a bachelor pad. I was excited about this plan because it would allow me to have my own living space but still be close to my parents if I needed anything.

One morning, I became curious as to how the construction was progressing. I was poking around the construction site when ten sheets of drywall fell on me. Pain shot through my foot as I struggled to free myself, but my foot was stuck, and I was unable to move. I stayed there for four hours in my PJs until the contractor found me and pulled me out. He called 911 before calling my mother. She rushed home just as the ambulance arrived. They took me to the helicopter pad on Gabriola and then helicoptered me to Victoria General Hospital.

The doctors determined that I had a broken bone in my right foot and fitted me with a cast. My dad drove down from Nanaimo and picked us up, and we went home. I wore the cast for ten days, and it took six weeks until I could walk properly with no pain and wear my shoes. Despite this somewhat shaky beginning, I would end up living in the carport-turned-bachelor-pad for the next nine years.

In 2006 I was hired at a local pharmacy that had a computer department; my job was to sell and fix computers. This was the perfect job for me. I felt like things were finally getting better after so many years of deterioration. I was good at the job too! I received three excellence awards, and customers got to know me by name, often requesting me because I was so knowledgeable.

Unfortunately, I was so good at my job that they gave me a promotion of sorts—or at least I'm sure that was how they saw it—into a sales-only job. I put in my resignation and got hired at a call centre. After a massive breakdown, I went back to my old job selling computers.

I took pride in fixing computers and customer service, but I struggled in the sales aspect. I always got extremely anxious when I had to deal with a customer. My anxiety started to increase as the store gave me more and more responsibility.

In February 2010 I started using a natural medication for my hay fever as my parents thought it would be better than something I got over the counter. For whatever reason, I had a bad reaction to this medication, and it increased my anxiety. I did not know at the time that I was having a bad reaction to it until it was too late.

I had been working at the pharmacy in the computer department for four years when I started to help myself to some of the petty cash. It was right there, so why not? You know, twenty dollars here, twenty dollars there. Who would ever notice? Well, they noticed pretty quickly, let me tell you.

If you haven't learnt by now, I am not a very good thief. I tend to act on crazy impulses, not planning things out. I knew that they had an overhead camera that looked down on the cash register, but I thought I could hide my actions from view. Boy was I wrong! My theft was caught on camera.

The theft prevention officer was brought in and, after reviewing the tapes, caught me red-handed. I was removed from my department and taken to the manager's office where the police were called, and I was arrested yet again and charged with theft under $5,000.

I instantly felt remorseful and told them I had Asperger's syndrome and to take that into account when they decided what to do with me. My employer had been good to me, and I had repaid them by stealing from them. Part of it was the reaction to the herbal medication, but I was also not taking responsibility for my actions.

I went to the police station and tried to get in contact with a lawyer but could not get a hold of anyone as it was Sunday. So, I left and went home and emailed my parents to tell them what had happened. They checked their email and found my message and then they soon phoned me and could tell I was right off my rocker, so they decided to call a friend who came over and saw how I was, and they called 911 for an ambulance. and I was admitted to the psych ward.

The psychiatrist on call that day was Dr. Joris Wiggers. When he saw me, I told him I was there for detox. I explained about my herbal allergy med and what had happened at work. He did some research and found that people prone to psychosis episodes were at a higher chance of having a breakdown with this medication, and that was what had happened to me.

My parents asked Dr. Wiggers if he would be my permanent doctor, and he agreed to take me on. He put me on a low dose of Risperdal to help combat the psychosis episodes. That was my first time back on meds in over ten years.

I once again appeared in court in April 2010. My employer asked the judge to allow me to pay back the money instead of going to jail. The judge agreed with my employer and included an order to write an essay on employee theft. If I did that, my charges would be dropped. My employer had known about my autism when I was hired, and they felt a criminal record wouldn't serve any purpose. I completed the essay and returned the money. Once again, my parents bailed me out by giving me the money I needed, as there was no way I could have saved up enough to pay them back in the agreed-upon time. Once the money was repaid, the store took me back. Of course, things were never the same again. I was hired back as a stock boy, but they continued to monitor me closely, not allowing me a job handling money. Not that

I blamed them. They reduced my hours down to four a week, which wasn't even enough for pocket money. I needed to find a job that would give me more hours, so I quit.

Next, I worked for an electronics store but was laid off after four months because my overall sales were too low. By this time, I knew I wasn't ever going to be an expert salesman.

In 2012 my nana had a stroke and my parents thought it would be a good idea for me to be her live-in care aide for a time. I would cook her meals, give her her medication, and help her around the house. This didn't last long as I couldn't handle the responsibility. My nana was mostly deaf, so she always had the TV up really loud, which bothered me and gave me anxiety. I was really sad to see her in her condition and wished I could have done more for her. I remembered all the family vacations we had gone on and how much fun we had together.

I had another stint in the psych ward; Dr. Wiggers treated me again. This was the first time I actually liked a doctor. He became a wonderful resource and advocate for my health and is still my psychiatrist today. He was also really the only one who, I thought, took a serious look at my medications and figured out the correct dosage for my drugs.

In 2013 I was still living in my parents' carport/bachelor pad on Gabriola Island. It was difficult to commute, so I wanted to live in Nanaimo to make it easier to find employment. My parents decided that I could live on my own, so they purchased a two-bedroom condo unit, and I moved back to Nanaimo. The condo was very close to the police and fire station—I'm not sure if that was intentional or not!

Moving into the new space was a challenge. I had a hard time adjusting to my new surroundings and it was difficult having my parents so far away. I was not well suited to living on my own without any family close by. I had support workers come in and check on me three times a week, but it wasn't the same. My anxiety worsened, and once again I felt myself spiralling downwards. Only this time there wasn't anybody around to catch me.

A while later, my parents decided to sell their home on Gabriola Island, and they purchased a condo in town for themselves. This was perfect! I told my parents I didn't want to live by myself anymore. I thought they would be overjoyed to have me back. Boy was I wrong!

They told me it would be better for my development if I continued to live by myself. Then they did some research and found a government agency that specialized in home share opportunities. We hadn't known about the existence of these home shares before. I didn't like the idea, but my parents thought this was great. The agency suggested that we consider bringing in a home share provider to live with me in my condo. We agreed to try it, and my dad stayed with me overnight until a provider was found and moved in at the beginning of November 2013.

My parents and the agency agreed this was a good plan and felt good about the direction things were going. The agreement was that my care provider would stay each night, cooking and helping me when required. Meanwhile, I was responsible for the bills and groceries. The care provider was able to continue with his day job if he held up his end of the contract. I didn't care much for this arrangement, but I reluctantly agreed.

I found a position as a cashier at a Target store that had recently opened in Nanaimo. The job was okay, though I hated selling Target credit cards. Target had massive expansion plans to move into the Canadian market, but unfortunately the large box store never really got a foothold. I stayed with them for about a year until the store went bank-rupt and I was laid off.

With the help of an employment agency, I was able to land a good job at the local library in Nanaimo, and I am still working there to this day. I put the books and other items away and sort the shelves. This is a great job for me and perfectly fits my skill set.

While I was living in my condo, I had another nervous breakdown and went to visit the psych ward. The doctors and nurses decided the medica-tion I was on wasn't helping, as I wasn't showing sufficient improvements, and I was put on new medication, Ativan, and Risperdal, which I had to take every day. Dr. Wiggers, who I was really beginning to like, initiated the change in my medi-cation. I felt he was the first medical professional to really take an interest in me.

Although my home care provider was supposed to help me, he pretty much left me alone, which I didn't actually mind because it meant that he wasn't interfering with my business. I'm sure he had his own issues to deal with, but I didn't really know since I tried to minimize contact with him as much as possible. I think he just saw me as an easy paycheque and free rent. One day this man just up and left me high and dry.

An emergency respite worker was hired until we were able to sort out this mess and figure out a new plan. I was still campaigning to my parents to let me move in with them, but to my surprise, they once again refused! I became increasingly angry and frustrated with them. I thought that they didn't want me, but I would learn later that they just wanted me to be independent and not always rely upon them.

Two government agencies met with me to figure out a plan of action. To their credit, they worked quickly to find a solution. I know that they felt bad about what happened to my last live-in aide and were determined to make things better.

They thought it best that I didn't live in the condo by myself but move into a home share provider's home. They told us they had somebody in mind that they wanted me to meet. I was dead set against this idea as it would mean more change, but I finally caved.

I met Dave, and at first sight, I didn't think we would be a good fit. He was a huge man with long hair and tattoos all over his body, and he was at least 250 pounds. He had a strong handshake and a deep voice. He could've easily fit in with any motorcycle club and could scare the crap out of a gorilla! Even before meeting him, I was determined not to like him and seeing him in person only soured my impression of him.

Dave had become an alcoholic during high school and stayed that way until he was twenty-seven years old when he sobered up after a hard night of drinking. He was a correctional officer before he had to retire for health reasons. Next, he worked in a recovery house, helping people through the first stage of alcoholism.

We met at Dave's house, and I had to admit it was very clean and nice, except for his antiquated television! I was sure it was from the dinosaur age. I thought a television was the most important part of any household, perhaps only beat out by the computer.

Dave had previously lived in Maple Ridge, never dreaming about moving to Nanaimo, away from his two children who he raised as a single dad. But then he spoke to a friend who said he would be a great home share provider. Dave talked about it with his two grown children and decided it was a good opportunity. Dave thought he would do a stint on the Island, earn a bit of money, and then move back to the Lower Mainland, but it didn't turn out that way.

All in all, it was an okay first meeting with Dave. Despite his scary appearance, he seemed like a nice-enough guy, but I still did not want to move in with him. Dave also seemed to think it was a good first meeting and thought we would be a good fit. But I wondered how my parents could even think about leaving me with this scary-looking man. And due to my experience with my last care provider, I was also very reluctant to try it again. I never told my parents any of this, however, and just slowly withdrew inwards.

My parents and I agreed to another meeting at Dave's house to discuss the matter. Dave put on his charm and my parents were convinced I should move in. Full of anxiety, we made plans for this crazy-looking biker to be my home share provider, even as I was planning on sabotaging the entire operation.

CHAPTER 5:
My Shaky Beginning

M Y PARENTS HIRED A local moving company to move all my belongings to Dave's house, which was located in a nice area of town, close to a lake. I still hated the fact that I had to move anywhere, and I resented the structure Dave put on me. He insisted that everything was clean and that I didn't drink any alcohol in his home. I wasn't much of a drinker, but the fact that there was a rule about it really annoyed me!

As I watched the movers pack everything I owned into boxes and put them into their truck, I became more and more anxious. It felt like they were slowly tearing strips off me. I felt as if my parents were once again abandoning me. As the day wore on, my mood became worse. I wondered how I was going to manage in the new surroundings and a new routine. I just wanted things to go back to how they used to be. No more changes.

Dave was kind enough to take in all my belongings from my condo even though he was only obligated to allow me to furnish my bedroom. This not only saved on storage fees but also made the house more of my place—not to mention it lowered my anxiety. After the movers finished, I stayed in my room. I stared at the wall. My head was spinning. Everything seemed so foreign to me. Again, I wished I was home with my parents, where they could take care of me. Why couldn't I just stay with them? I felt frustrated that they were making me go through this. Eventually Dave called me for dinner, and I ate as fast as I could. Dave tried to engage me in some idle conversation, but I did not say anything. I didn't want anything to do with him, and when I was finished, I retreated to my bedroom. I just wanted to be left alone.

The home was two storeys. A friend of Dave's lived in the suite downstairs with his dog. I tried to avoid this roommate as much as possible. He did not eat with us, and I didn't really interact with him. I wasn't pleased with his yappy dog. There was another roommate who had a disability who was also part of this home share agreement. His girlfriend would sometimes come over and eat with us.

For the first six months in my new home, I didn't do much except shower, go to work, and eat, trying to avoid contact with everybody. My anxiety kept building as I struggled to adapt to my new surroundings. Everything was so strange and foreign. I lived in my bedroom and only came out for meals, if I had to use the bathroom, or to take a shower. I could tell by his subtle hints that Dave wanted more interaction with me, but I would not engage him. I would not speak to anyone in the house unless spoken to and even that was a pain in the ass. Thank God I had a job that got me out of the "dungeon" three days a week.

Dave wasn't only a big man as I learned, he also had a big personality. He loved to talk, have fun, and joke, which really annoyed me. I tried really hard to convince Dave that I did not have a sense of humour. Maybe then he would leave me alone. I soon learned he was a pretty straight shooter. He would call things as he saw them.

Born in Quesnel, B.C., Dave moved east to North Bay, Ontario, when he was nine months old, where he spent the first ten years of his life. When his father retired from the Air Force, he moved back to British Columbia.

Dave didn't know much about autism, but little did I know at the time, he was researching and studying on the Internet to find ways he could help me. Dave was determined to show me that I could have a better life. I would learn he was also a keen observer and was quick to deduce things. When he had worked as a correctional officer, Dave was given a caseload of inmates to help and oversee. These skills helped him as a home share provider. Dave also understood the importance of teamwork and the giant amount of effort it took to change one person, to instill good habits and behaviours. He would use these skills to try and get all my health care professionals on board.

Despite everything, Dave did not stop trying with me, and kept trying to get me to open up, but every time I just shut him down. He was very patient with me, and for the first little while didn't push me too hard. He knew about my first home share experience and was intent on creating a more positive atmosphere for me so I could eventually thrive; I was more determined that this "experiment" would end in failure so I could go back to my parents. I did not want to live with this guy—or anyone for that matter.

I was just starting to get used to my routine when Dave announced to us that we were moving again. *Great, just what I needed.*

As the move date came closer and closer, my anxiety started to build and I began to have some minor meltdowns. A minor meltdown to me is heightened heart rate, sweating all over, minor shaking, brain fog, anxiety attacks, and hard time speaking. Dave was always supportive and helped me through them. He would talk to me in a quiet voice, let me be alone in my room, suggest that I listen to some soothing music and lie down.

To add to my high anxiety, I was laid off from my job so there went the three days of escaping from the "dungeon" and Dave's tyrannical rule of the household! It would be a full year before I saw another paycheque.

Dave and his roommate found another house to rent on the other side of town. For most people, moving isn't such a big deal, but for someone who has autism, I don't function well without a regular routine and consistency. While the new house was big and beautiful, I now had to get used to different bus routines and a new schedule. There was also a bit of a hill to climb whenever I came home on the bus, which I did not like. (I've well-documented my aversion to exercise in these pages.)

About a month after we moved, Dave sat me down and gently suggested that there would be some changes in the way things were run around the house regarding my routine. But what right did he have to tell me what to do?

He assured me that this was not an overnight process, and he would try to make it as seamless as possible. The first two changes Dave decided I would work on was spending less time in my bedroom, and I would do one household chore a week, which was cleaning the bathroom. Of course, you know what I said: "I don't know how!"

And how did Dave respond?

"No worries. I will teach you!"

I thought, *dammit, this tactic won't work!*

I would eventually learn that my favourite defensive tactic never worked with Dave. Most people would just get frustrated and give in, but not Dave! Oh, and one other minor thing! I had to leave my bedroom door open during the day when I wasn't home. At the time, I didn't understand why this was and I sure as hell didn't ask! Dave eventually told me how much better my room smelled by letting the air out.

A two-year lease was signed for the new house so I could relax a bit. However, I would fight Dave tooth and nail on his master plan to turn me into a functioning member of society. Having never really had any responsibility, I was beginning to understand how much hard work being an adult was.

Dave showed me how to clean the bathroom, and I did what he said, but did the least amount of work possible. At the time, I didn't know that Dave would go in behind me and finish the job. He would also clean the bathroom the weeks I missed. He did not say anything to me except once in a while he would hint at the spots I missed or that I might consider cleaning the bathroom more often than I did. He never really got too worked up for the times I missed my chores. His strategy was to slowly but constantly teach me how to act like a mature adult and make adult decisions. It would be a battle of attrition to see who cracked first! Sometimes Dave would kindly say that my middle name should have been changed to "stubbornly"!

Fortunately, my mom taught me to do my own laundry and maintain my bedroom. The problem was that I regressed and did not want to do my own laundry or take care of my bedroom. Because I liked to isolate, I would let my laundry pile up, overflowing my laundry basket. Dave would constantly suggest working "smarter not harder" and he suggested that I do my laundry once a week. As far as my bedroom went, it should have been nicknamed "Hurricane City"! Dave would hint occasionally to clean my room. Of course, I put the least amount of effort to show him that my way was best. I would justify this by convincing myself I never wanted to leave my room, and all the stuff made me feel comfortable. The fact of the matter was that I was just plain lazy, and in time Dave would point this out to me directly and provide a solution.

Dave had his tricks! He had a process that he was working on me.

Dave and my aide worker would meet once a month at the house and review my situation and discuss my goals and plans. This was one of the many ways he got me out of my room. He just kept telling me to trust the process.

Another trick Dave used, shortly after we moved, was to eat his dinner in the living room and leave me sitting across the dining-room table from the other man who I would not speak to; let's call him Jack. This went on for four months without either one of us talking to each other.

One evening, the man asked me from the other side of the table, "How did your day go?"

"Good," I said. End of discussion! But I think Dave saw that as a win.

But Dave would encourage me to talk by asking all sorts of questions. *WTF* became a constant expression in my mind when Dave would come up with a plan. Eventually I conceded that I would, in fact, have to talk to this man, so I carried on limited conversations with him.

My anxiety started to increase. With summer around the corner, still trying to settle down in the new house, and Dave continuing to push me outside of my comfort zone, I always felt out of sorts. I was also getting very anxious about not having another job yet. I had certain bills to pay, and things were getting tight financially. It just seemed I was in a constant state of worry, fear, and anxiety.

It was a beautiful, sunny evening in early June of 2015 when I had a huge setback. Dave had gone for a ride with a friend. Dave's other roommate—I will call him John—had also gone out, and the other home share individual Jack was at work, so I was home alone and completely out of sorts. While doing the dinner dishes, I took one of the sharp knives that I was washing and held it there for a moment, just slightly out in front of me. I stared at it for what seemed an eternity, and then I cut my wrist. I just wanted to see how it felt, so it was only a superficial cut. I admit I enjoyed the pain of the cut and seeing the blood as it dripped to the floor. I was confused because I did not want to die, but I was also tired of feeling anxious and scared all the time.

When I noticed the blood on the kitchen floor, I called 911 and told them I had just cut my wrist. The operator told me the police were on their way. I didn't move. To this day, I'm not really sure what went through my head. It was a kind of brain fog, as if I was disconnected or completely cut off from everything around me. Thankfully, within minutes I heard a knock at the door. Feeling lightheaded, I turned and answered the door. I didn't realize I was still holding the knife. The police officer rather forcefully instructed me to put the knife down. I did so, and they called an ambulance to check out my wrist.

Paramedics bandaged my wrist, and the police escorted me to the hospital where I was admitted to the psych ward for observation and evaluation. After three days the hospital staff wanted to send me home, but Dave said not until there was a full plan in place for future meltdowns. He also wanted a meeting with all the players to discuss options and treatments for my anxiety and autism. This is when I had to commit to start trusting the process and the plans for treatment instead of always fighting them. Although I was pessimistic at the time, I agreed to try the suggestions for my well-being.

I returned home ten days later, and this is when I took on a new way of thinking and started to trust Dave a little more. I saw he genuinely cared for me, and it wasn't just some sort of battle for control. Shortly after my return, Dave arranged a meeting between the agency and my parents. Dave wanted to discuss how I could become more self-sufficient and less reliant on my parents.

Since I had moved in with Dave, I had called my mom and dad at least once a day and texted them every day, sometimes two, three times a day. My parents were always patient with me and never brought it up as an issue. Dave, however, recognized how dependent I was on my parents—more so my mom—and wanted me to break free of this unhealthy behaviour.

Dave suggested that they devise a telephone system that would help break this dependency. My parents were on board with this idea. A decision was made by my parents, Dave, and the agency rep that I could only call on Monday and Friday— except for emergencies. I could only text once on Wednesday, Thursday, and weekends. I would meet my parents for hot chocolate on Tuesday;

therefore, no texting or phone calls were needed on Tuesdays.

Dave also wanted to cut down on sleepovers at my parents' house. I was going to my parents' house every weekend or every second weekend, and in Dave's estimation this wasn't helping my development.

When Dave told me this, I just about lost it. Who was he to try and control my life like this? Was he just trying to drive a wedge between my parents and myself so I would be more dependent on him?

What did he say?

"Trust the process."

I hated those words. I thought, *why is he being such a bastard!!*

I was always angry with him for trying to get me out of my shell, and the kinder and more patient he was, the more frustrated it made me.

I couldn't see that Dave was trying to help me. I didn't fully appreciate that Dave could recognize a little of himself in me. Dave didn't have autism, of course, but he understood what it was like to be afraid and to feel the world was against him. I was making a lot of decisions based on my fear, and Dave showed me how, if I made all my decisions based on this fear, it would be the wrong decision every time.

Dave also decided that I would spend less time with my parents, and that weekend sleepovers would stop, and any visits would be arranged beforehand. All parties—meaning Dave and my parents—agreed on this rule. This was a difficult adjustment for me, and I found it difficult to adhere to.

I continued to be admitted to the psych ward during my first four years living with Dave. Prior to the second stint, I called the crisis line from home and informed them I was going to harm myself. They asked me if I had a plan to hurt myself, and I said yes, I was going to slice my wrist. They remained on the phone with me until the police arrived and transported me to the hospital. The third occasion happened because I went straight to Dave and told him I wanted to hurt myself. He took me directly to the hospital.

Both stays were over the weekend, after Friday dinner, and this would become my pattern. I actually found some comfort in the psych ward, a sense of normalcy, a break from what I saw as Dave's unreasonable rules. Most people hate the psych ward, but I enjoyed the structure and the routine and found some strange comfort in the sterile surroundings. At the psych ward everything was planned for me, so I didn't have to do anything.

The reasons I gave for my behaviour were always the same. It was always low self-esteem issues and feelings of depression over my life and my autism.

Dave allowed this behaviour to continue, but he quietly documented everything, ready to present it to me as evidence. It was likely during the third or fourth time in the psych ward that Dave and the medical staff became aware of my pattern. I would return home after three days with a plan to get well and stop the meltdowns. Deep down I still thought I was hopeless and was incapable of changing anything. I tried to appease Dave and my parents by following the ground rules they had set out, but I thought that no matter how many rules they created I would still be the same.

Before we'd moved, I had arranged to find more employment with an employment agency, and I continued to check up periodically with them. Between psych ward stays, I wasn't doing much with my time other than spending about eight hours a week (over a three-day period) with my aide worker. He convinced me to go back to school and upgrade my English.

I enrolled at Vancouver Island University, and my first semester started in September 2015. I attended Monday through Thursday, two hours a day. With the help of my aide worker and Dave, I managed okay with transportation. I completed the first semester but dropped out midway through the second semester as I had secured a new job.

Other than my admittances to the psych ward, there were no other serious events, and in February of 2016, to my delight, I finally got back to work. Work often presented challenging situations, but making money was very important to me—I have very expensive tastes, so I've been told by just about everybody—so I tried as best as I knew how to control my anxiety.

My fourth meltdown happened shortly after I was hired at my new job, but it did not affect my work as I was scheduled Tuesday to Friday. Once again, I was home by Monday. These psych ward stays were inevitably what worked for me, and I was beginning to actually plan my meltdowns to happen on a specific day, at a specific time. Again, I didn't realize how closely Dave was watching me, and that he understood my behaviour to be a way to get a mini-vacation away from reality and responsibility. I tried just about everything to get to go to the psych ward during the weekends. One time Dave filmed me with his phone while I was having one of my psychotic episodes and played it for me after. Even I had to admit it looked fake.

At this time in my life, I had a counsellor, aide worker, psychiatrist, doctor, my parents, and Dave all trying to work a process with me. But I really believed I was smarter than all of them, so how could anything they came up with work in my "unique" situation?! They all told me I could actually control my anxiety and even stop it and get my meltdowns to a state of manageability. I started to wonder who really needed a psychiatrist!

All this time, Dave had been working with me around my hygiene habits, clothing issues, showers, and—without me realizing it yet—self-esteem. We had numerous discussions to help me deal with present-day challenges, or to introduce something new. For instance, I was taking thirty- to forty-five-minute showers and would only shower on workdays. I don't even like water touching me unless it's as hot as I can stand. I actually never once considered how my lengthy showers would affect others until Dave filled me in and told me I had to manage to get my shower time down to fifteen minutes. I would also turn on the fan for the full hour and had to break that habit as well. Dave was slowly showing me how self-centred I was in my behaviours. I would not even ask others if they needed to use the bathroom before I had my epic-long showers.

I truly was very self-centred and selfish in so many ways that I was blind to, and it really took a lot of patience from Dave and others to help me break so many habits. There would be three more trips to the psych ward between April 2016 and July 2017. Same old, same old pattern. The only difference was that one time, Dave decided the psych ward should keep me until at least the following Tuesday, and another one of those trips was a full week.

Dave knew that I would have to call work, and he felt this was a very necessary step in my growth, and that I needed to feel what it was like to be accountable for my actions. Nobody had done this to me before, and it was a bit of a wake-up call for me. Those were three of the toughest phone calls I had to make. Thank goodness my supervisor was a very caring individual who had told me on more than one occasion that health comes first.

In 2017 my nana passed away. This was a real blow as she was one of only a handful of people I felt I could count on. I went to see her in the funeral home. I knew this was probably a bad idea because it would likely cause another meltdown. Sure enough, it did, but I wanted to say goodbye. I remembered all the good times we had together, all the trips we went on, which I will always cherish.

My mother and I would make it a yearly ritual to go out to her gravesite and visit her.

Something that came to light at the beginning of 2017 was that there were conflicting issues happening with my outreach worker; let's call him Ed. My outreach worker convinced me to buy this very expensive remote airplane even though I didn't really want to. My outreach worker flew this plane and crashed it and then convinced me to pay for half of the repairs.

The outreach worker also claimed he had cancer and got a card to be able to buy cannabis and convinced me that I could also get a card to buy cannabis for my anxiety. At the time, the rules were that you needed a doctor's note—which was easy to obtain—to get a card in order to buy cannabis for medical purposes. Now, in Canada, it's completely legal, but at the time you had to jump through several hoops. I thought my outreach worker was just trying to be helpful, but what I didn't realize was that he just wanted me to buy weed so he could manipulate me and take my stash.

Dave had noticed a dramatic change in my behaviour and felt that I was withdrawing from life in general and resorting back to hiding in my room.

One day I bought some weed brownies and took them immediately to my room without stopping to say hello.

Dave thought this was very odd since I had made good progress up to that point. He came into my room and asked me how my day was going and what I was doing. Eventually, he asked what was in the bag.

I told him the truth—kind of.

"Brownies," I replied.

Dave said, "The only dessert you like is pie and ice cream. What are you talking about?"

I just shrugged. Whenever Dave would question me on anything it was like pulling teeth.

"Where did you get them?" Dave insisted.

"At the store," I again answered half truthfully.

Thankfully Dave let it go, although his BS meter was going off big time.

Over the last couple of months, my outreach worker had been pestering me to come live with him, so eventually I told Dave.

The outreach worker had told me that Dave was sick, and that it would be better if I came to live with him. Dave, never one to back down from an argument, called him up and confronted him.

"It's just idle talk," the outreach worker said.

"Really?" Dave said. "Because it sounds like you're borderline harassing him about it."

"Get your head out of your ass," the outreach worker said, and hung up the phone.

Dave called our agency rep, and she came to the house to get a full report. I sat down with the representative and Dave. I knew that Dave was really good at getting to the heart of the matter, and that this time I would have to tell him everything. Dave asked me if my outreach worker was smoking dope.

I dropped my head and said yes, he was.

Dave pressed on. "Does he do it in front of you?"

"Yes."

"And what about you? Are you smoking dope?"

I said that I was. I told him about how the outreach worker had told me I should get my own cannabis card so I could buy my own weed. I also fessed up about the brownies.

"No wonder you were messed up for the last couple of months," Dave said. "You know you shouldn't be taking anything with your medication."

In the end I was appointed a different worker and carried on with them, but this delayed my progress.

During this time, I had to see my psychiatrist at least every six months. After one of these visits, it was suggested that I consider some cognitive therapy, and I was referred to a woman who worked from her home in a town called Ladysmith, about twenty-two kilometres from my home. So, naturally I thought I would not have to do this because Dave would have to drive me there, wait an hour, and bring me back!

Wrong!

He said, "No worries. I will get you there."

Dammit. That had failed. I would try a different tactic.

"How am I supposed to find the money?" I asked.

"Don't worry. You can afford it," he said with a sly grin.

I decided Dave could win this round. I saw the cognitive therapist in Ladysmith about eight times, and I can say for the first time I felt a little hope. She introduced me to the latest tools that were being used in North America and other parts of the world to help with anxiety and autism meltdowns. It wasn't so much the hope that this would work for me, but that it might help others, and I could share with them. There were real ways to help stop anxiety and control meltdowns. I didn't actually believe it would help me, because I believed that I was unique.

She would assign me homework, including deep breathing, meditation, and something called the Distraction Method. This was a tool that would help me concentrate on something other than my anxiety. For example, I would have to name five electronic things in my house or name five things that were outside. I would have to write these down on a notepad each day, and I couldn't repeat myself in a seven-day period. This was a good tool when I was at work or on the bus where I couldn't lie down. All I had to do was look outside and distract myself from my anxiety.

At this time, I was in over one hundred Facebook support groups for autism and I would readily tell others about these techniques, yet I didn't want to practise them myself. I decided I was becoming the expert on autism, and they needed my guidance and direction. My ego was so huge that I actually believed I was becoming a medical expert.

In February 2017 I was on my computer and got a message on Facebook from an individual who stated that he could get me $250,000 from a disability tax credit I could qualify for. Great news! I went and shared this with Dave.

Dave tilted his head and stared hard at me. "Hold on there, buddy."

Dave looked at the message and he could clearly tell it was a scam. But I have always been driven to obsessive thoughts when it comes to money and thought this looked like an opportunity.

Dave even got on my computer and told the man where to go! Dave impressed upon me that this was a scam and the person on the other end was a crook and was taking advantage of my disability. The man was even dressed in an American armed forces uniform, standing in front of the American flag! I thought there was no way he could be lying.

"You can *not* qualify for a U.S. tax relief credit!" Dave told me.

But I wouldn't give up. I told my parents about the tax credit because what did Dave know, anyway! Unfortunately, they said the same thing as Dave. Still, I didn't listen and sent this guy all the money in my bank account to the tune of $1,200 U.S. using Money Mart. The man told me that he couldn't get the money, that there was something wrong with the money transfer, and I would have to find another way of sending it. It was getting late, but I went to put on my jacket anyway. Dave stopped me.

"What's up, dude? Where are you going?" Dave was a bit surprised because I had never gone out in the evening before. He thought I was making great progress. Little did he know!

"I'm just going out. Maybe bus over to the mall or something."

I thought if there was any chance I could get that type of money, I would do what it took and didn't care about losing my $1,200 U.S. I also really wanted to prove Dave and my parents wrong.

I took a taxi to Money Mart using my parents' taxi account so I could get the refund, and then took a taxi over to Walmart, where there was a Western Union. The woman at the counter told me that it was a scam and that I shouldn't do it, but I didn't listen to her either and sent the money anyways. No sooner had I gotten on the bus, I got an email from the guy who said he had gotten the money but wanted some more—just as Dave had said he would!

I told him that I had no more money. I had, after all, emptied my bank account to pay this guy. But the guy wouldn't stop pressuring me to get more money. He said I would get my benefit as soon as I made one more payment.

The next day I thought I had no choice but to tell Dave.

"I think I have a problem," I said.

"You *think* you have a problem?" Dave replied.

I told Dave everything. I was very angry with myself for falling for this scam. Why didn't I listen to anyone? Why did I think I always knew best? I was also angry at this man for ripping me off. This, of course, didn't help any of my self-esteem issues or my anxiety.

Dave continued to work hard with me so I would recognize my own faults in any particular negative situation. Previously, I would always look around for things or people to blame. It was never my fault! Of course, in my own stubborn way, I would push back against Dave and his methods. Dave told me I should take ownership and see how I contributed to the situation so I could then change my behaviour.

"Trust the process!"

Gradually, however, I began to see the wisdom in Dave's words. I have done a lot of work in this area, and I am now able to let go of my negative feelings. And part of forgiving myself is to promise myself not to repeat the behaviour. I am not perfect, but I am far better than I was.

With the help of Dave, the cognitive therapist, the psychologist, and the host of other professionals, life was beginning to calm down and get better. I had fewer mental breakdowns and was accepting this "trust the process" approach. Then—bang! We had to move again.

CHAPTER 6:
The Countdown Begins

W E HAD TO BE out of the house by the end of July.

I thought, *here we go again*.

The moving day got closer, and I could feel my anxiety increase as I struggled to control it.

Then one night, I was talking to my dad, and Dave asked me to ask him for a recommendation to a mortgage broker, as my dad had previously worked for a bank.

My dad suggested that Dave go see a woman in Nanaimo who used to work for him, who now had her own mortgage company. Dave told us he was going to see if he could possibly purchase a home so we would not have to move again. That would make me extremely happy indeed!

Dave was approved for the mortgage, and in July 2017 we had settled into our new house. It was a busy month, as the entire outside of the house was being renovated, and there was lots of commotion each day, which I did not like. However, I was glad to know that we would not need to move again anytime soon.

My therapy was going well, and I would use the tools I learned from the cognitive therapy sessions to fight against my anxiety. However, there were days when the anxiety would win. Thankfully, Dave had known me for some time now, and he was beginning to spot the tell-tale signs of my nervous breakdowns. They would be little things that I would do and ways that I would behave that would indicate that I was about to come apart. When Dave told me this, I of course didn't believe him. As someone with autism, I didn't understand the power of body language since I did not pick up on it myself. But gradually I realized that he was right, and my meltdowns were rather predictive. He would tell me to use the tools and exercises, which included lying down on the couch or my bed and listening to relaxing music. Still, at the beginning I wasn't great at it since I didn't put any effort into it and thought it was stupid and a waste of time. I wanted to prove to everybody that I was different and that nothing was going to help me with my meltdowns.

There are two types of meltdowns: the external type, which consists of the traditional temper tantrum—yelling, stomping, hitting, swearing, slamming doors, and just acting like a two-year-old having a moment—and the internal type, which consists of freezing up and shutting down. I almost never get the external type; I get the internal type. My heart starts pounding, I get chest pains, I sweat a lot, and I shake and get tremors or tics. I look down at the ground, have a hard time walking, have a hard time speaking, see all the mess everywhere, get a really dry mouth, and just become unresponsive.

Now I have found that I can distract myself with music and take my anti-anxiety medication as soon as possible, it calms me down and helps me to come out of the meltdown. I also do deep breathing and meditation exercises, and try everything to get myself out of the meltdown. My meltdowns last for hours even with all my efforts to get myself out of them, but they do go away eventually.

Back in 2012 I had tried to convince people on Facebook that I had Fragile X, which is a genetic

disorder characterized by mild intellectual disabilities. (It's a real disease, but I didn't have it.)

By 2017 I had probably diagnosed myself with at
least thirty other disorders. I don't even remember
all of them now. Unfortunately, the more I tried to
convince others, the more I started to believe in
this BS myself. It was just my way of feeling unique
and special and to give people a reason they should
pay attention to me. It was getting more and more
difficult to distinguish the true from the false.

Dave tried to help me through this, but by this
time, he also had his doubts about whether he was
the right person to help me. I had been making
improvements, but with the constant fighting,
Dave wondered if someone else would be better
at getting through to me. After all, Dave had never
dealt with anyone with autism before. Was it possible that there was someone out there who was
a better fit for me? He later told me he spoke to
several of his mentors who reassured him that he
was the right person to help me, so he stuck with
it. I guess he had to trust the process as well.

It was early fall when my behaviour began to
take on a more serious tone. Dave sat me down one
evening and presented me with numerous facts
about my phantom conditions, and it became very
evident to me that the gig was up. Dave showed

me all his observations over the last three years, and that I did not have any real pressing medical issues other than Asperger's autism and an anxiety disorder that was not as bad as I was determined to make it seem.

It was at this time that Dave informed me that we would strictly focus on getting my anxiety attacks under control to the point of stopping them and taking control of my meltdowns and control of my life. I had stopped counselling and journaling after we moved, and this did not go unnoticed by Dave when I thought it had. Dave told me I should start journaling again and that we would seek out a counsellor who specialized in inner child work and esteem issues. We set an appointment to see my psychiatrist and to get a recommendation for a counsellor.

The gig might have been up, but I wasn't going down without one last hurrah!

By this time, although I didn't much like what Dave had to say, I trusted him enough and gave him permission to review my daily journaling so he could help me keep it real and honest. He would impress upon me to express my feelings in my journal, but I really believed I did not have any feelings. Dave showed me that I did have these feelings and that I needed to learn how to express them, and he gave me many examples to work from. He reminded me to trust the process on many occasions and he reassured me many times that I could do what was asked of me.

My first appointment with my new counsellor would not take place until December 2018. I stayed diligent with the journaling, and Dave stayed just as diligent in reviewing my work. Somehow, I thought he would stop checking after just a few days. Thinking back, I suppose I should have known that Dave was even more stubborn than I was.

While my behaviour was improving, things were not perfect. Between autumn 2017 and 2018, I had three more visits to the psych ward. Once again, right on schedule. I had a meltdown Friday evening with the idea of coming home on Monday. The first two stays happened as planned, but I was in for a surprise on the last stint. By now, my pattern was extremely obvious to Dave, who never doubted for a moment that my weekends at the psych ward were all about me just escaping reality and not wanting to be accountable or responsible for my actions, health, and well-being.

I always made sure I had a good meal on Friday before I took another mini-vacation from life. Dave is a darn good cook, and hospitals aren't exactly known for good meals.

By now, though, neither my parents nor Dave dropped everything and ran down to the hospital to save me. This was part of my routine, yet I didn't even recognize it. Probably because I still felt everything was about me and sleeping away the weekends seemed ideal. Dave took my journal with us to the hospital and gave it to the staff to look at. This had never happened before either!

After my second-to-last psych ward stay, I returned home as usual and reluctantly carried on with my journaling, going on with life as if nothing was really going to change. I still thought that if I was difficult enough, Dave would eventually give up on me and leave me alone. I could not have been further from the truth! Dave persisted, and I dug my heels in for one last stand.

What I did not realize was that Dave's methods and processes were beginning to work despite my defiance. Sometimes I would be caught smiling or laughing at things I never used to smile or laugh at. I thought I had no sense of humour when I first met Dave and had no idea how to develop one. Every day, Dave, with his loud, boisterous personality, would encourage me not to take myself too seriously and try and laugh more. He would even joke about mistakes he himself had made and would laugh at himself, encouraging me to do the same. Dave would be quick to point out my positive changes and give me props every time I made a significant step forward. It has to also be noted that I was talking a lot more to my other home share roommate. He had a girlfriend whom I also had conversations with during her visits.

For the first time in my life, I was beginning to have... fun. After years of being bullied for my differences, years of anxiety, years of depression, I felt like the fog was slowly lifting. I felt that there was a path forward and it was becoming clearer with each day.

November 2018 would prove to be my last trip to the psych ward. Of course, I thought this would be another Friday-to-Monday excursion and back to my regular routine. The usual routine involved Dave driving me to the hospital, me checking into emergency, and then being admitted to the psych ward. Dave would walk with me to the ward, give me a hug, and leave. Not this time!

I was at the entrance to the ward with Dave when the admitting nurse looked at me and asked, "What is your plan?"

I was prepared for this question because they always asked me the same thing. "I'm going to slice myself in my throat."

"Are you going to hurt anyone else?"

I hesitated because I'd never been asked that before. I thought it would help me get into the ward if I said yes. I thought I had outsmarted them once again!

"Who?" the nurse asked.

This really threw me because I didn't know how to answer. I tried to reach into the back of my mind to come up with something. All of a sudden, I looked at Dave and pointed. "Him."

Although Dave took this seriously at the time, he thought it was pretty funny. We would later laugh at this incident, and I had to admit to the absurdity of it. How could I, a scrawny, uncoordinated guy, take on Dave, who weighed at least 250 pounds?

The nurse wrote my words down, and I was admitted. I was a regular there, and it kind of felt like a second home. All the nurses were very familiar with me by now too. Dave came into the ward with me and immediately asked to meet with the nurse who was appointed to my case. This had never happened before either. An hour passed, and Dave patiently waited to see the nurse. I even suggested he go home and try tomorrow, but Dave wouldn't hear it. He wasn't going to let me get away that easily.

My case nurse eventually took me and Dave to another room and that is when Dave filled her in on what had taken place since the beginning.

After listening carefully to Dave, the nurse turned to me and asked a single question that shook me to my very core. "When will you give up this game?"

I was in complete shock. How dare she? She didn't know what my life was like. She didn't know how the autism affected me. She didn't understand my anxiety or the pressure I felt on a daily basis! Sure, she knew my file and who I was, but she didn't have to live within my skin. She had no idea what she was talking about. But at the same time, deep down, I knew she was correct. My meltdowns weren't real meltdowns. They were just a way for me to avoid responsibility, to show people that I needed them and that they shouldn't ever leave me because I couldn't make it on my own.

I also knew that if I really wanted to try and make an effort, I could live a normal life. Without my knowledge, Dave told the nurse to have me ready to come home on Sunday and then he left.

Imagine my surprise when the nurse came to me after dinner on Sunday and told me that I would need to get ready to go home. What the hell was she talking about? It was not Monday! She then called Dave, and he instructed the nurse to have me waiting outside to be picked up. Dave arrived around seven o'clock, and I got into the car, and we proceeded to head home. Not a word from Dave. This was odd because you usually couldn't shut him up!

We got to within two blocks of home when Dave pulled over and stopped the car. This would be the turning point for me, the start of my complete surrender to the idea of changing the way I thought and the way I looked at my life.

Dave turned to me and asked me to tell him what was really going on inside me. I told him I did not know what he was talking about. Dave called bullshit on me and said he was prepared to drive around all night if that's what it took for me to become honest.

"You do know what is bothering you, and once you admit to the core issues, we will have something concrete to work with," Dave said.

I insisted I had no idea what he was referring to, and Dave again called bullshit and put the car into drive.

What was Dave doing? I just wanted to go home to play some video games and go to bed.

We'd only gone two hundred feet when I blurted out, "I feel as if I'm a burden to my parents and I don't understand how they could love me after all I've done to them."

For the longest time I hadn't realized the damage I had inflicted on them. How they had to deal with my meltdowns, how they had to rebuild the house, how they fought with the insurance company, how worried they were when I disappeared from the hospital, how scared they were that I would hurt them, and the millions of other things I did.

In the back of my mind, I thought one day they would realize I wasn't worth it, and then they would be gone. The only way to prevent that was to prove how helpless I was without them.

Dave looked at me for a moment. "Okay. What else?"

I looked down, unable to meet Dave's eyes. "I am nothing but a piece of shit."

"Finally," Dave said and drove home.

Those two hundred feet to the driveway felt like some of the longest in my life.

All along I had been blaming my autism for wrecking my life, when in fact it was my *own* thoughts about myself that were destroying me. What I had failed to recognize until that night was that this was exactly what Dave was trying to get me to concede to.

That night we sat down at home and had one of the best conversations I had ever been involved in. I shed real tears that night and made a firm commitment to myself to finally trust the process and go about making the necessary changes to become a much more positive, productive, and happy individual and to learn how to stop letting my autism rule my every move.

Dave was quick to remind me that this was by no means a quick fix and that patience and time would be my best allies. We decided to see the psychiatrist as soon as possible to find out if we could speed up the process.

Over the next few days, I reduced my Facebook groups from over one hundred to less than ten. My journaling stayed focused on how I felt about myself and my actions and my thoughts every day. Dave and I would continue to review it almost daily until he could see that I was being consistent and honest in my writings.

We were able to meet with the counsellor in December, and she set up my first appointment for January 2019. Dave taught me ways to get my anxiety under control. He gave me ideas on what to do at work when I would get panicky. I started to try some of the techniques and was quite surprised that they worked. I was able to stop anxiety attacks on the buses by simply deep breathing or focusing on some distraction. Dave seemed happy for me as I shared these experiences and would encourage me to keep on trying. Although changes were happening, I was still somewhat pessimistic about controlling any aspect of my autism. I had developed so many unhealthy habits; changing them seemed like an impossible task.

It was at my first counselling appointment that my counsellor suggested I try listening to music while lying down in my bedroom with the lights off during an autistic meltdown. I was not sure how this was going to help, but all I could hear was Dave saying, "Trust the process!"

From that day to this, I have used this technique and it has worked incredibly well except for one occasion where I came very close to a complete meltdown. Part of my meltdown routine was to lock myself in the bathroom but somehow, on this occasion, Dave was able to get me to go to my room and listen to my music. What has also helped is that Dave can now tell when I am about to have a meltdown and can tell me to go lie down and listen to my music. Before, I would always fight Dave and disagree with him, but not anymore. Sometimes I would just lie down, and I would be so relaxed I would fall asleep until the next morning.

The next step is doing this process completely on my own, without direction from others, on a consistent basis. (I'm still working on this one.) Sometimes it does not work right away because I give more power to the meltdown. On a couple of occasions, I tried to ignore Dave when he directed me to put my music on. I wanted to extend the meltdown, but Dave persisted, and I eventually gave in and went to listen to my music. My meltdowns have become less dramatic and less frequent than I ever believed they could!

My visits to the psychiatrist are back to every six months twice a year and may even be changed to once a year. I have every intention of making it without any more psych ward stays but have to take it one day at a time. My last visit was a medicine review where everything remained status quo. That was a first!

I also came to realize that my parents loved me no matter what, and they would never leave me. I had been angry at them because I felt they had abandoned me on so many occasions, but in fact they had done the complete opposite. They had actually empowered me! They were—and continue to be—my number one fans. Despite everything that has happened, their love for me is immense and I will always be grateful for their faith and trust and the potential they see in me.

Today I'm on a combination of Divalproex, Olanzapine, Abilify, and Klonopin, and have been on this combination for almost four years with very good results. This was achieved through the diligence and persistence of the psychiatrist and Dave.

I saw my counsellor bi-weekly for about a year, and she was instrumental in helping sort out my inner turmoil around low self-esteem and feelings of inadequacy. She helped me get past my childhood pain around the bullying and feeling different than others. She helped me see the difference between acting out as a scared little boy and an adult man. Between her and Dave, I have learned to trust my abilities to make responsible decisions and to do things that I had been so dependent upon others to do.

My counsellor felt her job was complete in December 2019, however if I feel a need to see her, I just need to call, and she will accommodate me.

While things have vastly improved for me, not everything has gone my way. I had a mild stroke in May 2020; I woke up in the middle of the night with a pounding headache. I went to the bathroom to grab some Tylenol, but in the morning when I woke up, I couldn't see very well. My anxiety began to skyrocket. I thought about getting out of bed but figured it would be better to just wait it out. Unfortunately, it didn't go away.

By early afternoon Dave called to me and asked why I hadn't gotten out of bed.

I eventually got up, stumbled out of my room to the entrance to the kitchen, and said, "I can't fucking see!"

"What?" Dave said. "Come to me and tell me when you can see me."

I started walking slowly forward, putting one foot in front of the other. I got within a foot of him before I could tell that he was there.

Dave phoned the hospital and asked them what the COVID-19 protocols were. They said that he would have to drop me off at the door and they would come out and get me. Dave said that was unacceptable and decided to phone 911 and ask for an ambulance to come to our house.

Dave told the 911 operator what had happened. The operator got me to hold out my hands, away from my chest. The operator then told Dave to get me to smile. Dave relayed this request. I tried but I could not smile on my left side.

Dave asked if the ambulance was on its way and the operator said it was.

We waited. The ambulance seemed to take forever and when the ambulance finally did arrive, my vision was even worse. The first responders got me to look at their instruments, but I could not see them. They took me to the hospital where they did some tests including a CAT scan, and it was determined that I had had a stroke.

My parents and Dave were freaking out, but I was relatively calm through the entire ordeal. It just seemed like another thing that could go wrong, and considering all that I had been through, I wasn't overly worried.

The doctors told me this was a rare occurrence, just one of those things that happened to people in my age group. They explained there was a vein that went down the back of the skull into the neck and this vein had two layers which had become separated and therefore there was insufficient blood flow to my brain. It wasn't related to my medication or anything like that and was more common than people realized. They told me there was a chance I might have another one, but it was unlikely.

The doctors gave me some meds and kept me there for two days before letting me go home. I recovered at good speed. My vision improved, but

I used a cane for a couple of weeks before I could see well enough not to need it. It was several more weeks before my vision was back to normal. My support workers took me for walks around the neighbourhood till my vision was back to normal. Thankfully, I have made a full recovery, although the experience was extremely scary.

Not counting the stroke, much has happened in these last three years that has allowed me to get to the best place I've been in quite some time—if ever. I realized that I could overcome all my doubt and negative talk and finally be myself.

I habitually thought negative thoughts on a daily basis and was extremely hard pressed to see any positive light in my life. So many days I did not want to live, so much energy put into believing I was helpless and couldn't do anything to improve my situation. I had become a victim of my own doing and had been very selfish and self-centred in all my actions and thoughts.

The first person to take a risk with me and point this out over time was Dave. I was angry with him at first and did not want to hear the truth. However, Dave was stern when I needed him to be, loving in spite of my behaviour, gentle sometimes, and most of all persistent in helping me get to where I am today. My beliefs today are drastically different than they once were. I believe in God today. I believe in myself today. I believe my parents, my friends, and my family love me unconditionally today.

All along, most people accepted me for who I was, and they accept me for who I am today. I was always the only one who struggled to accept who I was. I have come to learn that I can change whatever is not working for me, and there is always a solution to my problems.

Dave's three most used expressions throughout this have been "trust the process," "there is a method to my madness," and "there is always a solution!" He no longer has to prove this to me!

CHAPTER 7:
The Process Works

THIS ISN'T A HOLLYWOOD ending. I still have autism and anxiety. I still have my moments. I am by no means trying to suggest that I have cured everything or that my life is perfect. I *do* know that my life is far better than I ever dreamed it could be. I have changed and my life has changed—especially in the last three years.

When I first arrived in Dave's home, I was timid, scared, and full of self-doubt. I had no real social skills, didn't really care about others, and was a complete loner.

In 2019 I bought my parents dinner for the first time ever. While for most people this is something really small, for me it was a big deal. My parents were flabbergasted because I had never done anything like that before.

Before Dave, I had no real ambition other than to stay in my room, play games, and go to work for some pocket money. I could do very little on my own and relied almost entirely upon others to do things for me—simple things I could have done myself. Humour was nowhere to be found. I was angry at the world for the way it had treated me, until I learned that underneath, I was actually really sad and had not grieved. At one time I believed moving in with Dave was a horrible decision, but it turned out to be exactly what I needed.

I wrote this book with the hope to inspire others in similar situations, or those who are struggling to reach out and get the help they need. Despite my stubbornness and serious denial, I finally surrendered to the suggestions of another man, who does not have autism, but had demonstrated on numerous occasions the many ways in which we are similar. Despite the tough persona that Dave portrays as a biker, at one point we were both scared little boys ruled by fear. Dave had grown out of that fear and showed me how to do it as well.

Dave has had his own journey of recovery from alcoholism and has shared openly with me his own trials and tribulations. He does not take much credit for his recovery. Instead, he credits his mentors and friends who have helped him along the way. I heard a lot from this man, things that I had heard before from my parents and from others, but I had not listened to any of them. It was when my psychiatrist and my counsellor echoed many of Dave's suggestions that I came to realize all Dave wanted was for me to be happier and to become the adult man I was meant to be.

Before 2016 I was not involved in any social activity and would not walk on my own, except to the bus to go to work. I would not go to the movies by myself or without my parents. My mother was the only one who could cut my hair! I would avoid hugs or touching— even a simple pat on the shoulder. I had never bought a birthday or Christmas card or present for my parents—or anyone else for that matter. I would not say "I love you" to anyone except my parents, and even then, they always had to say it first. I did not volunteer to help out in the home and lacked cooking skills. I once told Dave I could cook, and he said cooking macaroni and cheese was not cooking! Touché! We laughed and laughed. At one point I would never have believed we would ever laugh together.

I used to go to the pool with my dad when I first moved into Dave's. I hated it and told Dave about how much I dreaded the experience. He asked what was stopping me from telling my dad about how I felt. I said I was afraid that my dad would be upset, and Dave said, "Then you are being dishonest with two people!" One of the many lessons Dave has taught me.

I eventually got up the nerve and told Dad how I felt and—lo and behold—he was okay with my feelings. He told me we could find something else to do that would make me happy. My dad reacted just how Dave had told me how he would react—there is a solution, indeed!

What a difference a few years makes! One night I was on the phone with my mom, and I told her I needed a haircut, and she said you better go get one then. Of course, I said, "I don't know how to do that."

The next thing I hear is Dave in the background saying, "Just go get a ^\$^\$## haircut!!"

I got off the phone and was ready to show Dave there was no way I could go on my own for a haircut. Dave then proceeded to lay out a plan for me and I went and got my hair cut on my own for the first time in my life. I was thirty-eight years old.

The barber now sees me about every six weeks. The barber treats me like a normal human being, just as Dave said he would. This experience has opened up a whole new world of possibilities for me. I couldn't believe that it was that easy.

After we moved in 2015, Dave suggested I take up Special Olympics five-pin bowling, an activity my home share roommate and his girlfriend were participating in. I said not a chance, but of course, Dave's famous stubbornness wouldn't let it go and he suggested I try it out for the next season. I stood my ground but finally conceded to try it in the fall of 2017. I managed to complete a full season despite the constant anxiety. However, I decided I wouldn't go back for the next season.

Dave and I discussed trying a different sport because bowling was too overwhelming. It was decided I would try bocce ball, and I would have been in my second season in the spring if COVID-19 hadn't hit and changed everything drastically. I really enjoy bocce and am eagerly waiting for all the COVID-19 regulations to end so I can resume playing.

There was another first, this time at work. I am training the new staff at the library on how to do their jobs. My bosses are now giving me responsibilities I never thought I would ever be able to handle. When I was working at the pharmacy and was given extra responsibilities, I had a meltdown.

Well, not anymore. Training the new staff isn't easy, but I'm handling it well!

There are four household tasks that I share with our roommate. I used to just do the bathroom and, as I'm sure you can recall, not do it very well at all. By the time we moved to our latest home I was doing the dinner dishes and cleaning the living room and kitchen. Our other roommate was doing garbage, recycling, and the bathroom.

The garbage and recycling were done once a week and Dave wanted the rooms done every two weeks. I definitely tried my very best to remember to forget to do my chores. Dave would remind us of and we would, of course, ignore him. We would compromise and do these tasks every Saturday until we were in the habit of doing them more routinely.

Our other home share roommate Jack moved out in February 2020 and I have taken on more tasks which I do every Saturday until Dave took on another home share roommate who moved in with us in September. He now does the dinner dishes while I do the bathroom garbage and recycling, and Dave picks up the slack.

These past three years have been full of firsts, and I am excited to have more. I went to my first evening movie by myself on the bus in the summer of 2019. This not only impressed Dave but my parents as well. I even went to my very first staff Christmas party. I was nervous because I knew I would have to deal with a lot of people and crowds, which I am not good at, but I didn't feel like I was going to have a meltdown. I even took the bus there and back! This was extraordinary because it was a dark night, and although I was feeling anxious, I persevered. I actually socialized with other staff. This was a brand-new experience, and I did not get overanxious about it.

I have purchased gifts and cards for my parents and others the last four years, as I have learned to become less concerned about myself and more concerned about others. I now know what it feels like to give to others. When I give to others, I get to see the joy on their faces, and you *really* can't put a price on that feeling. I am able, at times, to say "I love you" first to my parents, but it is still difficult to do. Dave assures me it gets better with time!

Dave has been such an instrumental part of my process. I couldn't imagine where I would be without him. Everybody around me has noticed how I have changed, and I'm especially happy at how I am able to interact with my parents. They have seen me through everything, the highs, and lows of my young life, and I really want to give back to them. At one point my mother texted Dave: "Thank you for giving us our son back." He told me about this text with misty eyes. This meant so much and just reminded us of our struggles with each other through the years.

Dave has a group of friends, a support group, some of whom visit or call on a regular basis, many of whom are his riding buddies. Dave has this strange nickname that all of his motorcycle buddies gave him: "Boomer." The story is that one day he was riding down in Washington State. He stopped to get gas, unlocked the gas cap, threw his keys into his saddlebag, went inside, and paid for the gas. He then threw his wallet into the saddlebag and took off, forgetting about the gas cap. Dave used to smoke and would light a cigarette every time he started to ride. But this time he knew he was going to get right on the freeway, which would quickly burn up the cigarette, so he decided he would wait to light one up.

When he got on the freeway, he felt liquid down his leg. He pulled over right away, realizing he had forgotten about the gas cap. He now had gas pouring down the engine, down his leg and onto the road. He killed the engine, put his kickstand up, put the gas cap back on, and wiped down the bike. He tried to do this before his friends realized he had stopped and came back to find him. But of course, he was too slow, and his friends swung around and asked what had happened. Dave tried to downplay it, but they quickly caught on and started howling.

"I'm glad I didn't light a cigarette, otherwise I would have blown my ass to kingdom come," Dave said to them.

From that time on he was called Boomer. Those are the kind of friends Dave has.

I didn't think I would ever get along with any of Dave's friends. About seven years ago Dave told me that his family and friends would treat me as a friend. I thought he was full of you-know-what! I didn't even know them that well. Why should they even care about me? But Dave was right, and now they all treat me like family. I will even hug most of them, or at least shake a hand. It's wonderful to feel like I have a group of people I can count on. There have been many times in this last year or so that I have had feelings that I *have* been able to express, with Dave mostly, but sometimes with other people—whereas before I would just bottle it up inside.

I have come to see the benefits in asking for help or talking out my problems. I am by no means perfect, but I am definitely a different man today.

Dave has been able to spend more time with me now on other areas of my life because he is not having to deal with the way I used to be—at least not nearly as often! For example, he has spent more time teaching me how to cook, and I completed my first unsupervised dinner. Dave resisted all the urges to come into the kitchen to rescue me. The dinner was a huge success, and Dave and I even posted it on Facebook! It is hard to put into words how much my self-esteem has improved, but so many things (like the dinner) have proven to me that a concentrated effort and honest self-appraisal on a daily basis does wonders for helping me feel good about myself!

Remember my messy room? One day Dave came to me and said I was showing how low my self-esteem was by the condition of my room. I had absolutely no idea what the hell he was talking about! I *only* had three separate garbage bags going, and I could hardly move for all the stuff on my floor—but besides that my room was clean! Dave suggested we reorganize my room so I would see what he meant. We spent an entire Saturday cleaning and organizing my bedroom, including hanging all my sports jerseys and pictures. What a difference that made! I have kept my room well-organized since then. Dave showed me how our surroundings can affect our moods.

Things are not always peachy, however, and I still slip up occasionally. At the staff Christmas party, I had a few drinks despite Dave's no drinking policy. I told my other roommate and he used it to get me to buy him smokes and extort money from me. He kept saying that he would tell Dave and I would get kicked out. Once he moved out, I told Dave everything—about my drinking and what the roommate had done. Dave said he was fine with me drinking a little as long as I did not cause a scene and it didn't react with the medication I was taking. However, booze was still not allowed in the house.

Remember Dave's tattoos? Well, I now have three tattoos of my own and am looking forward to my next one. When I asked Dave about getting tattoo work done, he said no problem unless my parents were against it. I got my parents' blessings and my first tattoo! I did not even flinch and got the outline and the colouring done in one sitting without crying. Dave was impressed with how I handled myself.

When I first moved to Dave's, you'll recall, I had a dog named Nemo. My parents kept Nemo because he did not play well with others. We decided to let Nemo come to our house for a visit in the spring of 2017 for a trial run. By this time Nemo was older and a little more irritable. During dinner one night, Nemo decided he did not like Dave moving his foot, so he nipped at Dave's big toe. End of test run!

When we moved to our current home, my parents asked if we would take Nemo, as I always had a dog in my life. Dave decided against having Nemo because of what had happened; he did not want to put others in that situation. I was truly okay with this and understood the reasons why. I would not have acted this way when I first met Dave; I would have kicked up a fuss and found ways to sabotage him.

Sadly, my parents had to put Nemo down in August of 2018. I keep a picture of Nemo and a box of his ashes on my headboard to remind me of the good memories I had with him. I really loved that dog!

We adopted a cat named Dora in the spring of 2018 and she took to us immediately. Recently we have been discussing the possibility of getting a puppy.

Unfortunately, I was laid off by the library in March 2020 because of COVID-19. This was difficult for me and could have sent me spiralling downwards, but it didn't. Thankfully, as things started to go back to normal, I got my job back in September 2020.

I have listed off my major firsts as my way of showing you that no matter how deep we let ourselves go—spiritually, emotionally, mentally—we can always recover our true selves through the trust of others, those who are truly concerned about our well-being and who offer to help without wanting anything in return. I had to trust the medical experts, counsellors, and mentors if I truly wanted to feel better about myself. I want to thank all who have aided me in this part of my journey. There are too many to thank by name and I am bound to forget someone. You all know who you are. I will, however, once again acknowledge my parents, whose unconditional love and support has allowed me to get to this place in my life. This is not over. I have adopted the attitude that I have been given a new beginning each day, and the choices I make when I wake up will determine the outcome of my day. I still have plenty to learn and am looking forward to each chapter of my life as it unfolds, one day at a time.

My life is no longer ninety-five percent bleak! My negative thinking has almost completely stopped, and I am far more optimistic about where my life is heading. Today, I pray for all those who struggle with themselves and hope that they find a path to recovery so that they may come to believe in themselves and, in turn, help others do likewise. Apart from my autism, what I really needed was to be free from myself. I was so wrapped up in my own head that I was blind to everything around me. My blinders have been removed; I have seen so much, and without a doubt have so much more to see.

CPSIA information can be obtained
at www.ICGtesting.com
Printed in the USA
LVHW040718100522
718380LV00002B/243

9 781039 128910